AUNT FANNY'S HOME,

AND

HER TALKS ABOUT GOD'S WORKS.

BY

THE REV. WILLIAM E. SCHENCK, D. D.

PHILADELPHIA:
PRESBYTERIAN BOARD OF PUBLICATION.
NO. 821 CHESTNUT STREET.

STEREOTYPED BY WILLIAM W. HARDING, PHILADELPHIA.

PREFACE.

THE simple aim of this little book is to afford its youthful readers some glimpses of God's wisdom, power, and goodness, as they may be seen in the commonest works of nature, and thus lead to deeper feelings of dependence on God, and gratitude towards him. In pursuing this aim the endeavour is made to cause the works of God and his blessed word to throw light upon each other. That God may bless the humble effort to the spiritual good of the youth who may peruse the book, and use it for his own glory, is the earnest prayer of the author.

PHILADELPHIA, 1863.

AUNT FANNY'S HOME.

CHAPTER I.

AUNT FANNY'S HOME.

IN a central part of the State of New Jersey, a few miles from a large and flourishing village, stands a pleasant old family mansion. It was built near the summit of a hill, so elevated that from its windows one might take a view over the country for miles around. From the house the ground sloped gently down into a lovely valley, through which, between highly cultivated meadows with here and there a clump of trees, a clear and rapid stream wound its tortuous way. Beyond this valley arose another hill, not quite so high as that on which the house was built. The more elevated portions of this opposite hill were covered with a forest, through which a gurgling rivulet leaped and wandered downward to the brook below. Indeed, the whole country around was diversified charmingly with hill and dale, with patches of wild forest and cultivated fields, and rocks, and streams.

Immediately around the house were beautiful grounds, not extensive, but planted with varied shrubbery, and laid off with winding and well-gravelled walks, the whole being always kept in the neatest possible condition. And altogether, without any pretensions to lordliness of style, this old mansion, with its neat, airy, and comfortable apartments, the carefully-trained vines and rose-bushes climbing its exterior, its well-kept grounds and shrubbery, and its lovely prospects over the adjacent country, gave one an idea that its owner possessed intelligence, thrift, easy resources, and excellent taste. Yet there was nothing of costliness or showiness about it. Thousands of such homes may be found in every part of our favoured land, especially in the near vicinities of our larger towns and cities.

The owner and occupant of the dwelling we have described was Miss Fanny Walton. She was a maiden lady, somewhere in that uncertain period of life for a lady, found between thirty and forty years of age. She was tall and erect in person; easy, polite, and vivacious in her manners; and over her face there was always such a flood of sunshine—she was so lively, so gentle, and so sweet in the expression of her countenance, that she might easily have been supposed to be much younger than she was. Miss Fanny was well known to all the poor in her vicinity, to whom in their times of sickness, or bereavement, or trouble of any kind, she was sure to come as an angel of mercy. She was a member of a Presbyterian church in the neighbouring village, where she was held by all in the highest respect and affection.

Miss Fanny had spent several of her early years at a boarding-school in the city of Philadelphia. Her mother had died while she was yet a child, and her father knew not what better disposition to make of her. She had, however, been happily placed in the hands of a pious and most judicious teacher, by whom her character had been, with the blessing of God, moulded to become such as we now find it. At the end of a few years the little girl returned to the paternal roof, a refined, cultivated, intelligent, and Christian lady. Assuming the entire charge of the father's household, she had refused several offers of marriage, and had with the most filial assiduity, watched over him for many years. A rapid decline had hurried him to the grave, and Miss Fanny, his only unmarried child, was, by his will, left in sole possession of the old homestead.

She was yet debating, at the end of a year after his death, whether she would continue to live thus alone, or whether she would sell the old mansion and farm, and go to live in the city where she had been educated, and where she had numerous friends and acquaintances. The struggle was a severe one. On the one side her life was painfully solitary where she was, and her friends urged her earnestly to come and reside among them in the city. On the other hand, she was strongly attached to the old home of her father, and of her childhood's happy days. Every room, and nook, and corner in the old house her heart clung to. And every tree and flower in the vicinity, every moss-grown rock, and every bend and tiny cascade in the babbling brook, she loved as a friend from which she could not resolve to separate. She had also a keen appreciation of the beauties of nature, and a susceptibility which intensely enjoyed them. She loved to gaze at the rising and the setting sun; to watch the pattering rains and the falling snow; to gaze upon the beauties of the landscape below, and of cloud-land above; to note the changes of the seasons from winter through the opening buds and flowers of spring, to the ripened harvests of summer, and thence on to the bending fruit-trees and brilliant forest colours of autumn. To her eye all nature was full of beauty and of joy, and she could not bear to think of giving up all these even for the sake of dwelling among dear friends in a pent-up city home.

While she was yet hesitating, Divine providence decided the matter for her. A widowed sister, who lived in a distant town, was suddenly removed by death, leaving three orphaned sons. Their father had left no relatives to whose care their training could be committed. The letter which brought to her the news of her sister's death, brought also an expression of that sister's dying wish, that Miss Fanny would take the little orphans under her care, and train them up for usefulness in the service of God. Her benevolent heart gave no slow or doubtful response to this dying appeal. Her decision was at once made to remain in her country home, and another week saw her three nephews domesticated in her dwelling.

They were fine boys—those three nephews. Although they had always lived in town, they were strong, active, and healthy lads, accustomed to much out-door exercise.

Willie, the oldest of the three, was about fourteen years of age, stout in form, and manly in his bearing. He had already made considerable progress in his preparation for college, and began sometimes to assume the dignity and lordliness of approaching manhood in his intercourse with his younger brothers.

Archie, the second, was a lithe little lad about twelve years of age. Although much younger and smaller than his brother Willie, he was as active as a young deer, and could beat him in almost any sport which did not require the exercise of mere strength. In mental and intellectual activity, too, he was fully his equal, if not his superior. He read a great deal, and remembered well and digested well what he read.

Samuel, the youngest, was between ten and eleven years of age. He was a quiet, pensive lad, not averse from a good romp in good company, but much disposed ordinarily, to seek retirement, and indulge in meditation.

Their aunt Fanny soon found that her nephews had had an admirable early training. Their mother had been a woman of devoted piety, and had well understood how responsible a thing it was to have immortal souls committed to her care by her heavenly Father.

Hence, she had put forth constant and earnest efforts to "train them up in the nurture and admonition of the Lord." She had taught them especially to love and to study God's holy word, and had accompanied her instructions with earnest daily prayer that God would bless it to their salvation. Her anxiety to have her sister Fanny assume the guardianship of her orphan boys, grew not merely or chiefly out of her anxiety that they should have a comfortable home and be well provided for in the things of this world. Her chief concern for them was, that the religious education she had begun to give them, should be carried forward after her departure to another world. And from what she knew her sister Fanny's character and piety to be, she was fully satisfied that she would have not only the intellectual qualifications for this work, but also the disposition to undertake with alacrity its performance.

Nor was she mistaken in cherishing this reliance. No sooner were the three boys domiciled in their aunt Fanny's home, than her heart began to yearn to make them happy, and to do them good. Not only were suitable arrangements made for them to receive regular instructions in the various branches of a liberal education, but she began to draw forth from her own rich stores of information, the means of cultivating their understandings and improving their hearts. While she led them to study largely and carefully God's own book, she also sought to make them see in God's works, spread all around them, the evidences of the Divine wisdom, greatness, and goodness. With much skill she led them to an understanding of the uses and benefits of the various natural objects which were always before their eyes, never failing at the same time to lead their thoughts from nature up to nature's God.

In this little volume we shall show to our young readers a few of the pleasant scenes occurring in aunt Fanny's home; we will accompany her and her three nephews in some of their pleasant rambles over hill and valley, in the forest and by the babbling brook; and will try to rehearse for their benefit some of the long and interesting conversations they had about the commonest things of nature, such things as my young friends who read this book will not be sorry, we hope, to know more about than heretofore.

CHAPTER II.

SNOW.

H dear!" said little Archie, "how black and heavy the clouds do look to-day. Now we shall have to keep indoors all day."

Boys do not love to stay indoors. They usually prefer much to play in the open air. It was no wonderful thing therefore that Archie said this in a somewhat impatient tone, and that his remark was followed by a fearful yawn. His words were addressed to his aunt Fanny. Now aunt Fanny was a very kind and gentle lady, and she had already learned to love her little nephews very much. She was very intelligent, too, and every day taxed her ingenuity and drew upon her stores of knowledge for means to make happy the motherless little boys left to her care. So, laying her sewing in her lap, as she heard Archie's remark followed by his yawn, she looked out of the window and exclaimed briskly:

"See, Archie, see, it is beginning to snow. How perfectly quiet the air is. How gently these flakes descend. Faster and faster yet they come. Now, boys, how would you like to have a talk about snow.

I think I could tell you some things about it, which would interest you very much?"

"Oh, yes! yes! aunt Fanny, do tell us all about the snow. That would be so pleasant this gloomy day."

"Well then, to begin, let me tell you that snow is just frozen rain. When the temperature of the upper air sinks below the freezing point, then the mist or rain that is up there, turns into snow as it descends. I say when that is the case in the *upper* air, for sometimes the air is much colder there than it is down on the earth's surface. So that sometimes snow descends when our thermometer stands considerably above the freezing point."

"Oh, yes!" said Willie, "I have often noticed that, and never knew how to account for its snowing at such times."

"When the mists and rain-drops freeze," continued aunt Fanny, "they display innumerable varieties of the most beautiful forms. Examined under a microscope they appear to be regular crystals. Scoresby, a celebrated Arctic voyager, examined a vast number, and has drawn the figures of ninety-six varieties. Here, in this little book, are a number of the most curious and beautiful. See how regular and graceful are their forms. They will remind you of the figures you saw the other day, when I showed you my Kaleidescope."

"Is'nt it wonderful, aunt Fanny?" said little Samuel. "Why I never dreamed the snow contained such beautiful figures. I shall never handle it without thinking of its beauty. I shall always feel sorry to walk upon it and crush these little crystals."

"My dear boy," said his aunt,

"if you would study them attentively, you would find all the works of God full of beauty in every part. But to return to the snow, these crystals are formed most beautifully when the air is calmest, and the cold intensest. Hence they are most beautiful in the Arctic regions. But did you ever see any thing, Archie, that was whiter than snow?"

"No, never, aunt Fanny," responded Archie, "why, when I have looked at the newly fallen snow, it has so dazzled my eyes that I could not afterwards clearly see any thing else."

"Just so, and therefore the Bible often uses snow as the emblem of the utmost conceivable purity. In this way it illustrates the indescribable holiness of the Lord Jesus, as you may see by looking at Mark ix. 3, and Rev. i. 14. There is a sweet and blessed promise made to all guilty sinners that if they will penitently accept God's offered mercy, their deepest and foulest stains shall be so completely washed away that 'though their sins be as scarlet, they shall be white as snow.' Isaiah i. 18. But I ask again, boys, did you ever read of any thing *whiter* than snow?"

The boys thought a moment, and then Archie exclaimed, "Yes! yes! aunt Fanny, I did. It was in the 51st Psalm, which I committed to memory a few weeks ago. The Psalmist prayed, 'wash me, and I shall be *whiter* than snow.'"

"Right, Archie, that shews the absolute and celestial purity which every sinful but believing soul will one day possess in heaven through the cleansing power of Jesus' blood. But now I will tell you another wonderful thing. Did you ever, boys, see any snow that was not white?"

"No, indeed!" exclaimed all the boys, laughing loudly.

"Yet we are told on good authority that in the polar regions the snow has been seen of an orange, of a salmon, and even of a red colour. This appearance is due to the growth in the snow of myriads of microscopic plants, each being in itself only a single cell. Snow storms have sometimes in high latitudes also presented a luminous appearance, so that every object has appeared to be covered with a sheet of fire."

"I have heard somebody say," remarked Willie, "that snow would make a knife rust faster than would any thing else. Is that true, aunt Fanny."

"Yes, Willie, I suppose it is in a good degree true. Snow-water has been found when analyzed, to hold in solution more oxygen than any other water. If so, it would undoubtedly be more active in rusting any metallic surface."

"But, aunt Fanny," said little Samuel, "what good does the snow do?"

"I am glad to hear you ask that question, my dear boy," said his aunt. "Well, snow is extremely useful in a great variety of ways. I will try to tell you some of them. In the first place, the snow falls in immense quantities upon the high mountains, and thence, by its gradual melting, it steadily and quietly feeds the springs, and through them the streams of running water which a heavy pour of rain would convert into fearfully destructive torrents, deluging whole districts of country. In many countries the snow upon the mountains, lasting far into the summer, tempers the burning heats, by cooling the breezes which pass over them to the plains below."

"Aunt Fanny," interrupted Archie, " I have heard a farmer say that there had hardly been snow enough as yet upon the grain-fields to cause a good crop next summer. What did he mean by that?"

" Why, Archie, the farmers, who are often shrewd and careful observers of the operations of nature, have found out that a good coating of snow, spread over their grain-fields in winter, protects the roots and tender leaves of the grain from the action of severe frosts. Throughout the temperate zones all vegetation is greatly benefited and protected thus by the snows of winter. It has been found that hardy Alpine plants, transferred to England, would perish even in the mild winter of that country, for want of their usual snowy covering. So you see, my dear boys, that the snow is very useful, as well as very beautiful. God sends it, as well as the rain and the sunshine, on a beneficent errand."

"That reminds me, aunt Fanny," said Willie, "of what I was reading the other day in the fifty-fifth chapter of Isaiah, where it is said, 'For as the rain cometh down, and the snow from heaven, and returneth not thither, but watereth the earth, and maketh it bring forth and bud, that it may give seed to the sower, and bread to the eater,'—and so on. When I read this I wondered what the snow had to do with producing seed and bread. But you have made it all very plain, and I now understand that verse better than before."

"Try always, my dear Willie, to search out the meaning of all that you read in the Bible. As God is the Author of the Bible, you may be sure that every verse is full of divine wisdom, and will well repay the most careful study. And now, boys, perhaps you are growing tired of this long talk. Look, the ground is now white with snow, and the sun is about to break through the clouds."

"Oh no! aunt Fanny," cried the boys, "we are not at all tired. It has been such a pleasant talk. We have learned so much about the snow, we shall always look on it with new interest. We are so much obliged to you."

"Well, now you can go out and have a little fun. I won't object to your having a good snow balling, if you will not make your balls too hard, and will play with moderation and in good temper. But the other day, when coming down the street, I saw a sight that made me feel very sorry. It was a large, strong, well-dressed boy, pelting mercilessly a smaller, weaker, and ragged boy with very hard balls. He had crowded the poor fellow up against a brick wall, and seemed to take a malicious enjoyment in really hurting and tormenting him. Never do such things as that, my dear boys. Remember that every hand-

ful of snow you grasp contains wonderful evidences of the wisdom and goodness of the Almighty Creator, and was sent to give happiness, not to cause pain. Be afraid and be ashamed to pervert what God has sent in goodness, to unkind and cruel uses. Now, go and play. Good-bye."

NOTE TO PAGE 29.—Some of this coloured snow was brought back from Labrador by Prof. Stephen Alexander of the College of New Jersey, and was exhibited for weeks in the office of I. S. Schenck, M. D., Professor of Chemistry in the College.

CHAPTER III.

AIR.

UNT FANNY," said Willie one day, when the boys, tired with play, had all taken their places in the cheerful family sitting-room, "Aunt Fanny, I have often thought of that nice long talk we had a month ago about the snow. And as long as the snow lay on the ground, I scarcely ever looked at it without remembering what you told us about it."

"I rejoice to hear it, my dear boy," said his aunt; "but you must not think that snow is the only interesting thing in nature near you. Every thing that God has made is full of interest to those who search into the properties and uses of His works. God reveals to us not only his power, but his wisdom, and his goodness, and many of his other attributes in these creations of his, which we daily see around us. Can you remember, Willie, any passage of Scripture which tells us this, and says that even the heathen might from his works have known much of God, if their hearts had not been so wicked as to mislead their understandings?"

"I think you refer, aunt Fanny,"

said Willie, "to a part of the first chapter of Romans, from about the eighteenth to the twenty-fifth verse, and more especially the twentieth verse, where it says, 'For the invisible things of him from the creation of the world are clearly seen, being understood by the things that are made, even his eternal power and Godhead; so that they are without excuse.'"

"Yes! that is it. So you see we ought to regard it as a duty as well as a pleasure to learn all of God we can, out of nature. It is true that God reveals himself far more clearly and fully to us in the Bible than in nature, yet the lessons of the latter, especially when studied in the light of the Bible, are very important, and may be made highly profitable. But now, boys, as you were pleased with our talk about the snow, suppose that while the sun is sinking so brilliantly behind those purple clouds, we walk out upon the lawn and have a talk about *the air*."

"Oh yes! oh yes!" exclaimed the boys, eagerly seizing their hats. "But what can you find to tell us about so simple and common a thing as the air?"

"We will see," said their kind aunt. "I think we could find enough in the subject to spend many hours in talking over. But we can only select a few principal and interesting facts about it. In the first place, can you tell me what the air is?"

The boys were much puzzled. They tried various definitions, but no one was complete and correct.

"Well, let us skip the definition, and get at the subject by recollecting that air is a fluid transparent substance which surrounds our globe. As the earth moves rapidly in its orbit around the sun, it floats, so to speak, in this sea of air called the atmosphere, which moves along with it, always surrounding it."

"Is it known," asked Archie, "how deep is this sea of air?"

"Not precisely, but it is supposed to be about forty miles in depth. It is deeper, however, or reaches farther up from the earth at the equator than at the poles. This is owing partly to the rotation of the earth causing the centrifugal force to pile up the atmosphere, and partly to the greater expansion of it caused by the sun's more perpendicular and warmer rays."

"Has any person ever been so high as that?" asked little Samuel.

"No, indeed, my dear," said his aunt, "no human being could breathe or live at a quarter of that elevation. For as one ascends from the earth's surface the air grows more and more rare, and at the same time colder. The highest mountains on the earth are only about five miles high, and the only other possible way of reaching a great height is by a balloon. In a balloon the ascension is caused by filling a large light ball, generally made of silk, with air or gas lighter than the lower atmosphere. When a man ascends a mountain, the cold becomes more and more piercing, and the peaks of the highest mountains, such as the Himmaleh mountains in Asia, or the Alps in Europe, are covered with perpetual snow. The same increasing coldness is felt by one ascending in a balloon. Can you tell me, Archie, what is the colour of the air?"

The boys all laughed loudly at this question. "Why, aunt Fanny," said they, "it has no colour at all."

"There you are quite mistaken, notwithstanding your laughter," said she. "The air is perhaps as nearly colourless as any substance we know of, yet it has a colour which can be seen when we look through great masses of it. Stop now a moment and look up into that cloudless sky overhead. Do you see any colour there?"

"Oh! yes, it is a bright and beautiful blue," said Willie, "that is the shade of blue generally called azure, is it not?"

"Yes. It is one of the most delicate and most charming of all colours. And it is susceptible of a countless variety of changes and shadings by the infusion of sunshine and of vapour or clouds. Hence the ten thousand glories of sunrise, and of sunset, and of cloud-land, ever shifting and ever presenting their magnificent views for our admiration. What a pity it is, my dear children, that multitudes of people so seldom look at the sky, and thus fail to enjoy these splendid paintings from the Creator's own hand. This is one way in which 'the heavens declare the glory of God, and the firmament showeth forth his handiwork.' Can either of you tell me what air is made of?"

Aunt Fanny's little listeners looked up at her as if doubting whether she were in earnest.

"Yes, what air is made of," she continued. "The air is not one simple substance but is a mixture of several ingredients. Its great bulk is composed of nitrogen and oxygen, which are significant names given to two gases by the chemists. There are also very minute portions of carbonic acid and other substances, but nearly four-fifths of the bulk of air is nitrogen, and nearly the remaining one-fifth is oxygen. Now it is very remarkable that while no animal can live if deprived of air, yet neither of these two ingredients when separated from the other will answer in the place of air. If any animal be placed in a tight vessel containing pure nitrogen it will at once die. It will not sustain animal life. On the contrary, any animal placed in a vessel of pure oxygen will die from an exactly opposite cause. Pure oxygen possesses too much life-giving power, it stimulates the vital functions excessively, and the animal dies from this cause. Natural philosophers, after making innumerable experiments with these gases, have reached this clear conclusion, that these gases, mixed in precisely the proportions in which we find them in the atmosphere, are in the highest possible degree, adapted to the support of animal life. You see then that just what human science and research have discovered to be best for us to breathe, God had provided for us from the beginning in the exhaustless profusion of this atmospheric ocean. May you never forget, my dear nephews, as long as you live, that every breath of air you breathe, contains in itself a most impressive proof of the power, the wisdom, and the benevolence of your heavenly Father."

"What you tell us is wonderful, aunt Fanny, truly wonderful," said Willie. "But is there no danger that in some way the proper proportion of oxygen may be diminished and so the whole animal world be reduced to suffering, if not to death?"

"No, my dear boy, so vast is the supply which God has made, and so wise and unfailing is the system of chemical compensations he has put in operation to replace all that is used up, or in other words so unfailing is his providential care of his creatures, that we need not fear any such catastrophe. The only real danger I think of at present

arises when a large number of persons are breathing the air of a very close room. The lungs of a healthy, full-grown man, inhale a bulk of twenty cubic inches of air at every inspiration, and he will use no less than fifty-seven hogsheads in twenty-four hours. About two-fifths of the oxygen is abstracted at every breath and sent into the blood. Hence, if a person sit long or sleep in a small and very tight room, he breathes the same air over and over, the oxygen is in a great degree exhausted, and headache and languor follow. You see from this the importance of having a sitting-room or bed-room well ventilated. When a large number of people are assembled, as in a school-room or a church, the importance of free ventilation is still more urgent. I will tell you of a dreadful occurrence which will illustrate this necessity. An hundred and forty-six prisoners were once confined for a night in Calcutta, in a single room only eighteen feet square. This room, afterwards famous as 'The Black Hole,' had no sufficient aperture for the entrance of fresh air. There was of course scarcely oxygen enough for the comfortable supply of one person. The unfortunate prisoners soon found themselves in a state of unheard-of suffering, which grew worse and worse every moment. In the morning, all were dead but twenty-three, and some of these afterwards died. Should God in judgment command the oxygen away from the surface of the earth for a very short time, all animal life, including our own, would be utterly destroyed.

"Aunt Fannie," asked Archie, "you spoke awhile ago about putting 'lighter air' in a balloon. Has air any weight?"

"Yes, Archie, it has weight, and its weight has been carefully ascertained. A celebrated Italian philosopher named Galileo, first discovered that air had weight. If a balloon be weighed when empty, and afterwards when filled with air, it will be found to have gained many pounds. One hundred cubic inches of air weigh thirty and one-half grains, or seven hundred and seventy cubic inches of air weigh as much as one cubic inch of water. This weight continually presses on every point on the globe, and it is this which causes liquids to rise in sucking-pumps, in siphons, and in the barometer. You will be astonished to hear that the weight of air which presses upon every medium sized person is about forty-two thousand four hundred and forty pounds."

"Ho! ho! aunt Fanny," exclaimed the boys; "why no man could possibly lift so many pounds, still less carry it about all the time on his shoulders. Why it would crush him into powder."

"Yes, so it would if it were any thing else than air. But here again the goodness and wisdom of God are manifest. He has made the air to be so subtle a fluid, and so elastic, that surrounding him on every side, and being even within him, the pressure is precisely equal in every direction, and hence he never even perceives it. Should you, however, take an empty bowl, and after turning it upside down upon a table, succeed in pumping all the air out of it, so as to make what is called a vacuum, you would find yourself not strong enough to lift that little bowl you had so often handled. The reason would be, that the air having been removed from under it, the whole weight of the atmosphere would come upon its outside. And could you so place a man as to remove the whole weight of the air from one side of him, and to leave it on the other side, every bone in his body would be crushed to atoms."

"Dear aunt," said Willie, "what a mercy indeed it is that the air is made so thin as to find its way to every place, and thus brace and sustain us at the same time it presses upon us. I thought the snow was interesting and wonderful after you told us what you did about it. But I now think the air a thousand times more so."

"We have but touched, my dear Willie, upon a few of the more interesting points. When you come to study Natural Philosophy and Chemistry, you will learn a thousand wonderful things about the air, which we have not time now to speak of."

"How glad I shall be to study those branches," said Archie. "I wish I could begin them right away. But I want to ask you to explain to us something said in the Bible. Why, aunt Fanny, is Satan called 'the prince of the power of the air?' He is so called in Ephesians ii. 2. The verse is in my Sabbath-school lesson for next Sabbath."

"I am very glad, Archie, to see you trying to glean knowledge out of every subject to help you to a better understanding of the blessed book of God. I hope you will do so as long as you live. Many opinions have been held in regard to that designation of Satan. Satan is, however, frequently spoken of in the Bible as the chief or prince of the fallen angels, having authority and control over them. And it is equally clear that these fallen angels or devils move invisibly through the atmosphere, busy in the work of tempting and destroying human souls. In God's inscrutable wisdom he allows Satan and his angels thus to have liberty to rove about through the regions of the air, doing all the mischief he can over the whole earth. So that when you look around and see no one, you ought never to forget that even through these wide tracts of balmy and refreshing air, Satan and his subject hosts are always prowling about, 'seeking whom he may devour.' There is no safety save in a loving trust in the Lord Jesus Christ, who is ever near us, and whose power is infinitely greater than that of Satan."

"And now, dear boys, it is time for us to go in. The sun has sunk behind the western horizon, and night will soon be here. But look once more at those gorgeous clouds, piled one upon another like vast mountain ranges. The scene reminds me of one predicted in the word of God, and which each one of us will be sure one day to see. I mean the judgment-scene. Then Jesus, the blessed Saviour, shall come visibly among the clouds of heaven. Upward through this blue air 'every eye' shall be turned to gaze upon him. And while they who pierced him by their sins, unrepented, shall wail because of him, all who shall have believed upon him will be gathered in one grand assembly around his shining throne. Earth will be able to afford no plain broad enough—no arena vast enough for that countless concourse. Therefore, when the 'dead in Christ' shall have 'first' risen, then they 'which are alive and remain shall be caught up together with them *in the clouds*, to meet the Lord *in the air*.' These wide-expanded fields of azure ought to help keep us always mindful of that solemn scene which shall hereafter be presented when in their blue depths the throne of judgment shall be set, and that vast assemblage gathered there. May you, my dear boys, so live lives of faith on Jesus and obedience to his will, as to be all found gathered safely then to his right hand."

CHAPTER IV.

WATER.

HROUGH the valley stretching away to the eastward in front of aunt Fanny's house, there flowed a beautiful little river. Into this, from the hills on the other side, descended a rivulet, leaping over many a cascade, and singing many a sweet gurgling song upon its way. There, where the winding rivulet glided along with its delicious music, under densely overhanging trees, was a favourite resort for aunt Fanny and her boys. Here we find them one bright, sunny afternoon, sitting upon the dry grassy bank of the brooklet. From their cool retreat they could look down into the valley and trace the course of the shining river below, far, far away towards the point where it emptied into the deep, broad sea.

"Did you ever think, my dear boys," said aunt Fanny, as they seated themselves around her on the grass, "what an exceedingly important and precious gift of God is *water?* How indispensable it is to man, every day and hour of his life! How essential it is for the uses of commerce, for every branch of manufactures, for agriculture, for every department of human industry? Unless we should except the air we breathe, I think it would be very hard to name any greater or more important gift bestowed upon us by our Creator in all the works of nature."

"Yes, aunt," said Willie, "I was trying to think of that some days ago, when I was walking near the river, and I meant to ask you at some future opportunity in one of your nice talks, to take water as your subject."

"I am glad to hear what you say, Willie," said his kind aunt. "It encourages me to hope that I may have stimulated your thoughts into greater activity upon this class of subjects. Never be content, my dear boy, to let your aunt, or any other person, or any book, do all your thinking for you. Try to do your own thinking. Get knowledge from persons, or books, or observation, or wherever you can, but try to combine anew the items of knowledge you collect, to reflect upon them often, and to draw fresh inferences from them for yourself. It is only by such a process you can become a truly intelligent man. Without it, however great may be your store of knowledge, you can only be a book-worm, perhaps even a numskull. But let us return to our proposed subject."

"Before you begin, aunt, please allow me to ask you one question.

When I was thinking about water the other day, I remembered your telling us that air was compounded principally of two gases, and I wondered whether the same was true of water. Is it so, aunt?"

"Yes, Willie, it's just so. Water is made up of oxygen and hydrogen, each of which alone is an invisible and impalpable gas or air. The proportions of these elements in water are, one volume or bulk of oxygen to two of hydrogen, or by weight, eight of oxygen to one of hydrogen. I will here mention one curious fact. Hydrogen, when alone, is highly inflammable. If set on fire, it combines with oxygen from the air, and what kind of ashes do you think it leaves? The result is *water*. Is it not singular, that the fluid we usually regard as the peculiar antagonist of fire, should be formed by the action of fire? And as water can thus be made, so there is an easy way by which it can be unmade. You have only to lay a piece of iron in a vessel of water. Yery soon rust will begin to form upon the iron, and that rust is only the oxygen of the water cntcring into combination with the iron. The iron steals away oxygen from the water and solidifics it, and twico tho bulk of the oxygen thus stolen becomes pure hydrogen gas, ceases to be water, and disappears in the atmosphere. A chemist could show you a thousand curious and instructive experiments with water and its components. But my object at present is not to instruct you in chemistry so much as to suggest some things about water, adapted to show God's goodness in this his important gift."

"I shall never forget," continued aunt Fanny, "having once heard Gough, the temperance lecturer, eloquently apostrophize a glass of pure water which he held in his hand. It seemed like a new revelation. I have never seen a glass of pure sparkling water, from that day to this, without thinking how beautiful and how precious a liquid it is. It has been both truly and poetically called, 'the wine of Eden.' Indeed, there is no wine in the world to compare with a sparkling glass of fresh spring water. And then, boys, what a blessing it is to have it to drink in such plenty. Were we compelled to use any other beverage, such as wine or cider, or even milk, as much as we do water, we should very, very soon become most heartily tired of it. Besides that, it would very soon produce the most injurious effects upon our health, both bodily and intellectual. But fresh water is always wholesome, never hurtful in any way. We continue to drink it day after day, year after year, and its only tendency is to promote health and lengthen life. We ought to bless God every day for the refreshing draughts of this precious beverage.

"And then, too, how plentifully has God furnished to us this precious refreshment! From every hillside and valley he has made it to gush forth in copious springs. In rivulets and brooks and rivers he has caused it to flow everywhere for the free use of man and all the lower animals."

"Yes," said little Samuel, "even the busy bee and the tiniest fly can always find water. How much water God has made for his creatures. Is it so all over the world, aunt Fanny?"

"Yes, my dear boy, everywhere except in those comparatively unimportant portions called deserts.

Such as the great Desert of Sahara in Africa, and the Arabian Desert in Asia. Why it hath pleased God to withhold his supplies from these spots of our globe, we do not fully know, but it is well for us to note the effect of his doing so. And when we see how the mere lack of water can change a country into a parched, barren, and almost impassable wilderness, where neither plant nor animal can thrive, or even live, it ought to make us the more deeply thankful to God for having given to ourselves and the whole race such copious supplies."

"I have often wondered," said Archie, "why it is that the rivers and especially the springs never run dry. There they are, their streams

running, running, running on, and have been, I suppose, for thousands of years, and yet they never get empty. Why is that, aunt Fanny?"

"Because, Archie, God has provided an immense reservoir, and has so ordered the operations of nature that the fountains and the streams are filled from that reservoir, just as fast as they flow. Where does all the water go to, Archie, that flows from all these fountains and streams?"

"Sooner or later," said Archie, "it finds its way into the ocean."

"Yes," said aunt Fanny, "and the ocean is that mighty reservoir to which I have referred. The sight of even a little speck of ocean, or a hand's-breadth of it comparatively, is enough to fill one with awe by a sense of its vastness. Oh how well do I remember, when I was a very little girl, to have once climbed with my dear old grandfather to the top of a lofty promontory which jutted out over the very waves. Many were the deeply interesting things he told me as we sat there for hours, about the sea, and the rocks, and the birds, and many other things. But I could scarcely keep my attention fixed, my soul was so filled and oppressed with a sense of the mightiness of the ocean. And yet all I could see was but a most insignificant little piece of it. For, do you know, boys, that very nearly three-fourths of the whole globe is covered by the ocean with its bays and gulfs and seas."

"But," said little Samuel, "how does this big ocean keep the rivers from getting dry? How does the water get back again to the springs after it has gone into the ocean? It cannot turn around and run up hill again."

"A very important question, my dear little fellow. I will try to answer it. God causes the warm sun to shine upon the ocean. The warmth causes the water to rise continually as vapour from its surface. The winds and gentle breezes sweep these vapours far away in different directions over the land. Sooner or later they become clouds. Then they come in contact with cold currents of air, or with the mountain-tops. They are condensed by the cold into rain-drops or snow-flakes, and down they come, to run again in due time, into the springs and rivers, and then back to ocean. So you see there is a continual compensation. The ocean is continually giving back through the atmosphere in snows and showers, what the land is giving to the ocean through its rivers."

"It is truly wonderful, aunt Fanny," said Willie. "And I very well remember when uncle George made us his last visit, that he took me with him one day to the tip-top of the mountain on the other side of the valley yonder. While we stood there he explained this very thing to me, and pointed out to me how, while the river was running towards the ocean all the time, the clouds were that very moment driving far in upon the land, before

the wind. And I remember his telling me, too, how God in his infinite wisdom and goodness so ordered it, as to make just about as much water go back upon the land as ran out to sea. He said that if God should send back too much we would have destructive floods; if he should send back too little we would have terrible droughts, and then the grains and fruits of the earth would perish, and men and animals must suffer dreadfully. As it is, uncle George said, God very rarely allows us to experience either calamity severely, only just enough now and then to make us remember that He is the Author of all our mercies, and how easily he could withhold even the commonest of them if he chose."

"I am rejoiced, Willie," said his

good aunt, "that you have so well remembered what your uncle George told you. It encourages me to hope that you will remember my words also. But, my dear boys, it is already beginning to grow late, and we have as yet gone but a very little way into our subject. We will now return to the house, and if we are not disturbed, will resume the subject in the evening. It is my fervent prayer for you all, that these talks upon the incessant and beneficent workings of God's power and goodness, may lead you truly to love and to trust him. Remember, what one of our hymns so sweetly says, 'He who fears God, has nothing else to fear.' He holds all the powers and elements of nature under his supreme control, and he has promised that he 'will make all things work together for good to them that fear him.'"

CHAPTER V.

WATER.

SCARCELY was the tea-table cleared in the evening, when the boys began to urge their kind aunt to resume the interesting conversation of the afternoon. Accordingly, after attending to a few necessary arrangements for the household, she took her arm-chair, and occupying her busy fingers with a piece of knitting-work, remarked:—

"While we were taking our tea, I observed an exemplification of a natural law in relation to fluids, to which I will call your attention before passing to other matters. While pouring out your tea, I noticed that the tea always stood at the same level in the spout of the teapot as in its main body. This reminded me that it is an exceedingly important fact in regard to water, that through whatever tight channels, and to whatever distance conducted, it will rise in them as high as the fountain head. It is by the action of this law that most large cities are now supplied with water. In Philadelphia, for instance, the water with which the city is supplied from Fairmount, is elevated by pumps worked by water-power, to a reservoir on the top of a hill. From this reservoir, pipes pass under the ground to every portion of the city, and to almost every house therein. These pipes may be carried up to the highest stories of tall houses, and the water flows freely through the pipes up to any point not more elevated than the reservoir at Fairmount. Thus water may be carried in pipes from one mountain to another, under deep intervening valleys. And whenever it is desired, an escape may be provided for the water through a short branch tube, when it will spirt high into the air, forming a beautiful jet or fountain."

"But, aunt Fanny," cried Willie,

"if that is so, why did the ancients build such vast and costly aqueducts to bring water into their cities? I was reading very lately, a book of travels, in which the magnificent aqueducts built to lead water into various Grecian, Roman, and Oriental cities were spoken of and described. What was the use of building these along mountain-sides, and across deep and wide valleys on lofty arches, if they could have led the water along the surface of the ground through pipes?"

"Your question is well-timed, my dear boy," said his aunt. "There was no use whatever. Had they known as much about this matter as is now known, they would have saved themselves a vast amount of labour and expense. But in ancient times they understood very imperfectly, if at all, the law to which I have adverted, that water when confined will rise at any distance to the level of the fountain-head. You see here, boys, a new proof of the value of natural science. And I hope you will be more ready than ever to be diligent in its acquisition."

"Indeed, I shall, aunt Fanny," exclaimed Archie. "And the next time I go to Fairmount, I shall look with more respect than ever on the water-works, and the great reservoir on the hill, and even on the great ugly iron pipes. But now, aunt Fanny, I want to ask you why it is that people often die of thirst upon the ocean? I have often read about ship-wrecked people who were in great distress for water to drink, even while floating upon the waves?"

"I will try to tell you, Archie, with pleasure. The water of the ocean is very far from being pure. It contains a number of ingredients, such as salt, soda, lime, magnesia, and sulphuric and muriatic acids, besides vast quantities of decomposed animal and vegetable matter. These substances give to it an intensely bitter taste, and when it is swallowed, cause it, instead of quenching thirst, to create only a far more intense and tormenting thirst than before. Yet even here we see God's goodness. For were it not for the salt and other substances found in it, the vast ocean might become a vast sheet, from which foul and poisonous vapours would carry pestilence and death abroad over the earth."

"Thank you, aunt Fanny. But I want to ask another question, if you please," said Archie, earnestly. "When I went with you to the seaside, last summer, I found it much easier to swim in the salt water than it is in the fresh water of our river. Why was that?"

"It was, Archie, because those admixtures I have just spoken of, made the salt water much heavier than the fresh, and of course it was correspondingly difficult for your body to sink into it. The water of the Dead Sea—that monument of wrath—contains one-fourth of its weight of salt, iodine, bromine, and other substances in solution, and travellers tell us that a man can hardly get entirely under its surface, even when trying hard to do so."

"Oh! aunt Fanny," shouted Samuel, "I heard Biddy say something so funny the other day. It was washing-day, and Biddy said to the cook, that the water in her tub was so *hard* she could scarcely wash with it. I thought at first it must be frozen into ice, but the weather was too warm for that. What did Biddy mean, aunt Fanny?"

"Well, Samuel, I suppose Biddy

herself could not very well have explained what she meant. But the term *hard* is very often applied to water containing some chemical compound of lime in larger quantities than usual. This lime decomposes the soap which is used in it, and thus prevents it from having any cleansing effect. But *hard* is a strange word to apply to a liquid, sure enough, my boy."

"I have often wondered," said Willie, "how it is that a fish can breathe in the water. Won't you tell us, aunt Fanny?"

"I cannot go into a full explanation, Willie, for it would take a long time. This much, however, I can easily tell you. All water which is long exposed to the atmos-

phere, such as spring or river water, absorbs a considerable quantity of air. The breathing apparatus of the fish is adapted to separate this air from the water. By the help of its gills, after having taken in a quantity of water through its mouth, it can eject the water and retain the air."

"When uncle George was here, aunt Fanny," cried little Samuel, "he went a fishing one day, and pulled a beautiful great fish out of the brook. Little cousin Emma tried to hold it, but it flounced about so, she could not. It appeared to be in great pain, and to grow weaker and weaker, until at last it was dead."

"That was because God, the All-wise Creator, had adapted its organs to breathe in the water, and there only. When drawn out of the water, there was such an excess of air as to overpower it and destroy its life. Poor thing! I hope you pitied it. And I hope, dear boys, you will never wantonly inflict pain on any creature of God. To catch fish for food, I consider allowable, but to catch them only to sport with their sufferings, is very cruel.

"But while the fish could not live out of the water, one of you boys could not live in it, and for the same general reason, because God has formed you to live and breathe on dry land. A few years ago, I was visiting at a beautiful town on the banks of the Susquehanna. A poor lad had fallen from the deck of a boat and been drowned.

I happened to pass by just as his body had been brought to the bank, and laid on the grass under the large trees. It was a sad, sad sight. But you see, my dear nephews, since sin has come into the world, death has followed it. Now, every one of those elements which was created by infinite benevolence, and contains in itself so many sources of blessing to mankind, may easily become to him a source of pain and death. All this has been deserved. God now speaks to us, you see, every where in his works, in mingled tones of goodness and of wrath.

"In God's blessed word, water is used as an emblem of a variety of sweet and precious things. Can either of you repeat to me any delightful invitation of the Old Testament, in which salvation by Christ and its attendant blessings are offered under the image of abundant water?"

The boys thought a moment. "Oh, yes, yes, aunt Fanny," cried Willie, "in Isaiah, chap. lv. 1, is the invitation, 'Ho! every one that thirsteth, come ye to the waters.'"

"Very well. Now, Archie, where is there a similar invitation in the New Testament?"

"In the last chapter of Revelation, 'Let him that is athirst come. And whosoever will, let him take the water of life freely.'"

"Right. And there are many other such. Now when you think how abundant is the supply of water furnished to man and beast, what countless springs, and never-failing brooks, and noble rivers, every where give opportunity to slake one's thirst, never forget that just so abundant and so without price are the blessings of salvation which God offers in his Gospel to every poor sinner. The worst and wretchedest sinner on the face of the earth need not perish. Let him accept God's free offer, and he will live and be happy for ever. Whenever you see an exhaustless fountain or a flowing river, try to remember this.

"Water is also a divinely appointed emblem of the Holy Spirit in his sanctifying and refreshing influences. Under this image, the Saviour promised the presence and indwelling of the Holy Spirit

to his disciples. To the woman of Samaria, at Jacob's well, he said, 'Whosoever drinketh of this water shall thirst again, but whosoever drinketh of the water that I shall give him shall never thirst; but the water that I shall give him shall be in him a well of living water, springing up unto everlasting life.' John iii. 13, 14. 'Jesus stood and cried, saying, If any man thirst, let him come unto me and drink. He that believeth on me, as the Scripture hath said, out of his belly shall flow rivers of living water. But this he spake of the Spirit, which they that believe on him should receive.' John vii. 37–39. Every true believer would find this world but a dry and thirsty

desert indeed, if the Saviour did not fulfil this promise to his faith, and, at the same time, refresh, and cheer, and sanctify him by this blessed gift of an indwelling Spirit. In these promises, what a precious significance has our Saviour given to water, by thus making it an emblem of the Divine Spirit. Can you tell me, Archie, what terrible punishment God once inflicted on this world by the agency of water?"

"You refer to the Deluge, aunt Fanny," replied Archie, "when God caused the whole earth, even the tops of the highest mountains to be overflowed, and all mankind drowned, except eight persons whom he saved in the Ark."

"Aunt Fanny," broke in little

Samuel, "you were telling us this afternoon, that the deep ocean covered three-fourths of the world, and how much water there is besides in the rivers, and the clouds, and everywhere. Now, if the people should get very wicked again, would not God send another deluge to destroy them, as he did in the days of Noah?"

"He could do so, undoubtedly, my dear boy. His infinite power is adequate to do it whenever he would. But we may rejoice in knowing that he will not. He has given us an express promise that there shall no more be a flood to destroy the earth. And in token of this promise he has set the rainbow in the heavens. Gen. ix. 11–15.

Whenever you see that brilliant arch in the sky, remember that by it God is saying to all mankind, 'Be not afraid. I remember my promise. I will never permit another Deluge to come upon the earth.'

"It is now growing late, and we must get to sleep. But there is one thing I will add which will perhaps increase your interest hereafter in the subject of our conversations to-day. It is this:—An extraordinary number of the miracles recorded in the Bible were wrought by the agency of water, far more than by any other element. Let me just remind you of a few of them. Moses turned the water of Egypt into blood. The same prophet afterwards divided the waters of the Red Sea, and made them stand up like walls on either side as the Israelites marched through. In the wilderness, he converted bitter waters into sweet. He smote a hard rock, and a stream gushed forth and followed the host, supplying them with drink upon their weary march. The waters of Jordan were divided before Joshua, as the Red Sea had been before Moses. Elijah prayed, and God sent fire from heaven, which licked up the abundant water he had poured upon and around his altar. Elisha cast salt into the fountain at Jericho, and its waters were changed from bad to good. The same prophet caused an iron axe to swim upon the surface of a stream. The first miracle of Jesus was the changing of water into wine. He commanded the stormy sea, and its waves were immediately hushed into a calm. He walked upon the water as safely as upon dry land, and enabled the apostle Peter to do likewise. But I have not time to mention others. Do you remember, Willie, any mention of water as being found in heaven?"

"Yes, aunt Fanny, there are such mentions of it in several passages; especially is it thus spoken of in the book of Revelation. Here is one which I learned in Sabbath-school some time since. 'They shall hunger no more, neither thirst any more, * * * for the Lamb which is in the midst of the throne shall feed them, and shall lead them unto living fountains of waters.' Rev. vii. 16, 17. And here is another from the description of the New Jerusalem. 'And he showed me a pure river of water of life, clear as crystal, proceeding out of the throne of God and of the Lamb.'" Rev. xxii. 1.

"Very well. I am glad you have such texts in your memory. Water, then, may remind us of salvation, both as begun here on earth, and completed hereafter in the skies. Here, they who believe on Jesus Christ, enjoy draughts of 'living water.' But these are foretastes only, yonder they may approach the '*river* of the water of life' and drink at will forever of its abundant flow. My dear boys, may you never look again upon a fountain or a stream of water without remembering these very precious truths."

CHAPTER VI.

FIRE.

THE evening was chilly, and the wind whistled shrilly around the corners of the house. The Autumn was not far advanced, but so cold had been the afternoon that a blazing fire had been kindled on the hearth. As aunt Fanny and her nephews turned away from the tea-table, they were not sorry to cluster around the cheerful blaze, and derived from it a feeling of unusual comfort. When they had quietly settled themselves in their positions, Willie remarked with animation,

"Aunt Fanny, you have told us many surprising things about air and water, but it seems to me that fire must be one of the most interesting things with which we are familiar. Won't you lay aside your book this evening, and talk to us about fire?"

"With pleasure, my dear Willie. I think we shall find fire one of the most mysterious and remarkable of the things we daily see. And I fear that I shall be compelled to pass over many of its most wonderful qualities and phenomena, lest I take you deeper into the science of chemistry than you are yet prepared to go. Even the most eminent chemists and natural philosophers have found themselves unable to this day to answer many questions in regard to the exact nature and origin of this powerful agent."

"Oh, please skip all the hard things which have puzzled the scholars, aunt Fanny," cried Archie, "and tell us such things as we can easily understand."

"Very well, Master Archie," said his aunt, tucking him good-naturedly under the chin, "we shall try not to overtask your youthful wits.

"Fire is probably, next to water and food, most absolutely and universally necessary to man. He needs it to defend himself against cold, to cook his food, to forge his utensils, and for innumerable other uses. Hence it is one of the first and most important of all agencies in aiding the advance of civilization. But while in ten thousand ways fire acts the part of a most useful servant, it sometimes proves itself a terrible master. Did you ever see a house on fire, Willie?"

"O, yes, I remember once when I was in New York, there was a terrible fire in the evening. I ran thither with uncle George. There was a crowd gathered around a burning house. At an upper window appeared a poor woman, almost crazy with fright. She was at last safely rescued, but it was by hard work. The flames roared and

crackled and whirled through and around the house terribly."

"Persons are not seldom burned

to death. Vast quantities of valuable property also are often destroyed by fire in large cities. Hence the formation of fire insurance companies, by which device any loss is divided among a large number of persons, and is heavily felt by none. Hence, also, the invention of the fire-engine, worked usually of late by steam power, for the extinction of conflagrations. The improvement in these has in recent times been so great that they can ordinarily very soon extinguish even a large fire. But in past years New York and Philadelphia, and other large cities, have suffered severely. In the year 1666 a great fire occurred in London, which burned over thirteen thousand houses. The flames at one time formed a column a mile in diameter, and seemed to reach the clouds, while its effect upon the sky was visible even in Scotland. The most terrific work performed by fire, however, is when it destroys a ship at sea. Then, especially if the weather is at all tempestuous, there is ordinarily no escape for crew and passengers from sudden death. Some of the most thrilling tales of human peril and loss of life the world has ever read have been narratives of ships destroyed by fire at sea."

"Aunt Fanny," said Willie, "I not long since read of a people somewhere who worshipped fire. Will you tell us about them?"

"Yes, Willie. The brightness and beauty of fire, and its benefi-

cent yet terrible power, caused it to become, at an early day in the world's history, an object of veneration and worship. The first distinct sect of fire-worshippers arose in Persia, where they were called Guebres, and spread through India, where they are called Parsees. They are a people peculiar in their habits and customs. Their chief distinguishing characteristic is that they worship fire, in which they find an image of the incomprehensible God. They offer their prayers before a holy fire, which they maintain burning uninterruptedly on their holy places. This holy fire they say their great prophet Zoroaster kindled four thousand years ago."

"I have read of fires taking place which no person had kindled. Do you think such a thing is possible, aunt Fanny?" said Archie.

"Yes, Archie, it not seldom happens. Certain substances exposed to the action of the atmosphere undergo chemical changes by which they may be set on fire. Even living persons may be exposed to this danger. There are reputed instances in which the bodies of drunkards have become so saturated with alcoholic spirits as to take fire apparently without cause and be burned to death. Such occurrences are called instances of spontaneous combustion."

"I heard two men talking one day," said little Samuel, "about a sort of fire they called a 'Jack-o'-lantern.' What do you think it was, aunt Fanny?"

"It is an appearance, my dear

boy, said to be sometimes seen in low grounds. It may be caused by the spontaneous or accidental combustion of some gaseous substance arising from decayed animal or vegetable matter. Sometimes this flame is borne along and swayed up and down by a breeze, so as to give it the appearance of a lantern carried in some person's hand. This appearance formerly was, and indeed is even yet, a source of great terror to ignorant and superstitious persons. It has been variously called 'Jack-o'-lantern,' 'Will-o'-the-wisp,' and '*ignis fatuus*.' I trust, my dear boys, you will never allow your minds to be degraded and held in bondage by any such superstitious terrors."

"In the history I was reading not long since," observed Archie, "I found that fire was used in England and Scotland for making signals at the approach of an invading fleet or army. Piles of dry wood would be prepared on every conspicuous hill-top along the boundary or sea-coast, and a man stationed by each pile ready to fire it in an instant. No sooner was one fire kindled than that on the next hill-top blazed up also, and then the next, and the next, and so on for hundreds of miles, and thus all the people knew that the enemy was approaching."

"That was the telegraph of those ruder days, Archie. Those fires were called beacon-fires. The same was anciently done in Palestine, on the approach of the Feast of the Passover. On the proper evening, appointed persons climbed the Mount of Olives and kindled a great heap of faggots. This blaze could be seen afar off. Then another and another blaze would appear, and so they would extend from one mountain top to another, until all the land was illuminated, from Olivet to Lebanon. This was the signal announcing that the time for celebrating the Passover had come."

"What is meant, aunt Fanny," inquired Willie, "by the expression of passing 'through the fire,' so often used in the Scriptures? The Jews are said in several places to

have made their children to pass through the fire, and it seems to have been some great crime of which they were guilty."

"It was indeed an awful sin. Jehovah is the only true God, and he was by solemn covenant the God of the Israelites. But they often forsook him entirely, and worshipped the gods of the surrounding heathen nations. Among these was Moloch, a false god worshipped by the Ammonites. To this god human beings were offered in sacrifice, and to him the apostate Israelites offered as sacrifices their sons and daughters. Diodorus Siculus, and after him the Jewish Rabbins, tell us that the image of Moloch was made of brass, and seated on a brazen throne. The head was that of a calf with a crown upon it. The throne and image were made hollow, and a furious fire was kindled beneath it. The flames ascended into the form of the idol, and when the body and arms were red-hot, the poor victim was thrown into them and thus burned to death, while its cries were drowned by the beating of drums. Truly, heathenism hardens the heart and brutalizes the nature. To this day you know how in India widows ascend the pyres and are burned alive with the bodies of their dead husbands. And the sentiment of the heathen community causes the widow to be despised and shunned who shrinks from such self-immolation. How true it is that the only safety of man is in knowing the true God, and keeping his commandments."

"Yet wicked as are those Hindoos, aunt Fanny," observed Archie, "I have never thought them half so bad as were those professed Christians who took good men and women, and burned them at the stake. I not long ago read 'Fox's Book of Martyrs,' and it is horrible to think of such cruelties as were practiced on good people only for reading the Bible and worshipping God in their own way."

"Yes, Archie, some of the most terrible scenes in the world's history are those connected with the Christian martyrs. The wickedness of those who inflicted such tortures and deaths was vastly aggravated by the knowledge of God's will they had, or might and ought to have drawn from his holy word. Yet the early history of Christianity is filled with records of these dreadful persecutions of the saints of God. On one occasion, after a great conflagration in Rome, it was given out that the Christians had set fire to the city. Thereupon the cruel Emperor Nero caused large numbers of them to be seized and smeared with pitch and other combustible materials. They were then tied to stakes in the public gardens and squares and set on fire.

"Then in later centuries came the terrible persecutions of the true children of God by papal authority. Men and women, the young and the aged, were dragged before the tribunal of the Inquisition. By the application of cruel tortures, confessions were sometimes extorted from themselves or from other witnesses. They were then usually bound to a stake, faggots were piled around them, and their bodies were burned to ashes. Many thousands of devoted Christians were thus murdered in the times preceding the Reformation. The world will never forget the names of John Huss, Jerome of Prague, and many other noble men who thus died for conscience sake, going up to heaven as in a chariot of fire."

"Aunt Fanny," inquired little

Samuel, "where does the fire in the volcanoes come from?"

"That is not an easy question to answer with certainty, my dear Samuel," said his fond aunt, patting him on the head. "The most commonly received theory is that the whole interior of our globe is a mass of liquid fire, and that the gradual cooling and contraction of the earth's exterior causes this liquid fire to issue violently through the apertures found in these volcanoes. It is supposed the entire globe was once a ball of fire, whirling along in its orbit. As the outside cooled very slowly, it formed a crust, growing thicker and thicker, upon which vegetable and animal life were afterwards called into being. This supposition seems to be confirmed by the fact that the deeper we descend into the bowels of the earth, the warmer the temperature becomes. The existence of many warm springs, such as the geysers of Iceland, is also cited in support of this theory.

Some men of science have ventured the assertion that this crust is not more than a hundred miles in thickness, scarcely thicker, in proportion to the earth's diameter, than is the shell of an egg to the egg's diameter."

"O dreadful!" exclaimed Willie. "Why, aunt Fanny, suppose this crust should one day somehow be broken or crushed in, what would become of us and all living creatures on the earth's surface?"

"Of course all would perish, Willie, without some special exertion of Divine power in our behalf. But we are always and everywhere necessarily dependent on God, the Almighty Creator and our Heavenly Father. We must learn to trust him in all things, and he has graciously promised that all who do trust him shall ever be safe under his protecting care. There have been those who supposed that the final destruction of the world would be brought about in some such way as you just now supposed. Indeed, the Bible seems to teach us plainly that fire is to be the great agent in accomplishing that purpose of God. The Apostle Peter says, in his second epistle, chap. iii. 10, that 'the elements shall melt with fervent heat, the earth also and all the works that are therein shall be burned up.' But, as I have said, we ought not to be terrified by such a contemplation, but only be incited more earnestly to put our whole trust in Jesus Christ, our Divine Redeemer, and to keep God's commandments."

"I have often noticed," said Archie, "when reading my Bible, that God is said to reveal himself in fire. It seems to make him very terrible. Why is this so, aunt Fanny?"

"The fact is as you have stated, Archie, and I am pleased with every new evidence that you read your Bible with careful attention. Fire seems to be a most fitting emblem of the Divine justice. God's appearing in fire is a warning to every sinner that God is a God of infinite justice, and that if he relies only on that justice it will destroy him for ever, just as fire would consume his body. Hence he appeared as a flame of fire to Moses in the burning bush, and descended on Sinai to deliver the tables of the law, surrounded with thunderings and lightnings. The fire which consumed the sacrificial victims upon which sins, typically transferred, were confessed, indicated the same solemn truth. And so, when the day of repentance and of mercy to the finally impenitent shall have passed, we are told that even the Lord Jesus shall appear to them in 'flaming fire, taking vengeance.'"

"Do you suppose, aunt Fanny," said Willie, "that in the eternal world fire will really and truly be made an instrument in punishing the lost, or are those passages which so represent it, to be figuratively understood?"

"Many of the most terrible passages in God's word represent the lost as enduring everlasting torments caused by the fierce agency of fire. Thus Isaiah the prophet puts the solemn question, 'Who among us shall dwell with the devouring fire? Who among us shall dwell with everlasting burnings?' The Saviour speaks of them that go down to hell as passing 'into the fire that never shall be quenched,' and elsewhere as being driven from the judgment seat 'into everlasting fire prepared for the devil and his angels.' These words are fearfully significant of the keenest sufferings conceivable. Whether literal fire will be employed in the infliction of eternal retribution has been a subject of much controversy. But man combines in himself two natures, a corporeal and a spiritual. Both are in this world made the subjects of divine judgments. Corporeal as well as mental pains are inflicted from God in punishment for sin. And we can see no reason why it may not be equally the case in the place of despair. The body after the resurrection will no less than the mind be made a vehicle of anguish to the finally lost. The whole subject is full of solemn warning. My earnest prayer is, my dear boys, that you will all give such heed to God's threatenings, as well as to his gracious offers of pardon and salvation through Jesus Christ, as to escape that anguish and secure a place in heavenly happiness. Meanwhile, may each of you be able to see such significance in these threatenings, that you shall never look upon a flame of fire without offering an earnest prayer that Jesus in his infinite mercy may pluck you, a poor hell-deserving sinner, 'as a brand from the burning.'"

CHAPTER VII.

LIGHT.

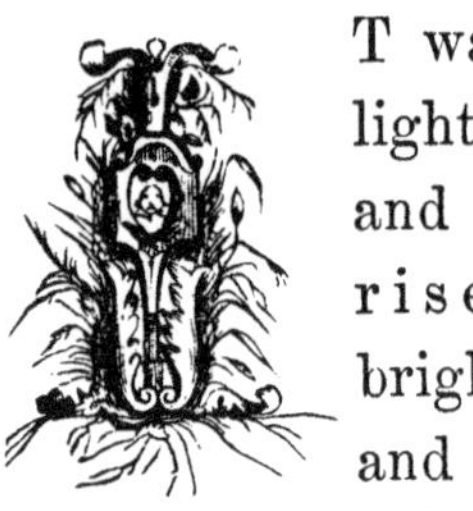

T was one of the delights of aunt Fanny and her nephews to rise very early, on a bright, clear morning, and take a ramble over the beautiful country in the vicinity of their pleasant home. It is wonderful that so few persons living in the country turn these charming hours of early day to any good account. People in large cities have a tolerable excuse for lying in bed later, but in the country, where the rising sun, the green fields, and the songs of the birds may be made to add so much to the pleasure of life, they who fail to make good use of the early hours, lose a choice portion of their existence.

One morning early, as our little party strolled forth, the sun was just peeping above the horizon, the birds were already singing gaily, the golden clouds were scattered over the eastern sky, and the variegated lights and shadows were lying in charming intermixture over all the landscape.

"Did it ever occur to you, my dear boys," said aunt Fanny, as they walked along, "to how great a degree we are dependent upon *light?* I think it not improbable that, enjoying it so profusely and constantly, you have scarcely ever inquired what light is, and how many benefits we derive from it."

"No," said Archie, "I don't think I ever did. Will you not tell us, aunt Fanny?"

"It is a question easier asked than answered, Archie. Natural philosophers have speculated and written much upon the subject, but I doubt whether they have ever reached conclusions in regard to the nature of light quite satisfactory to themselves. Some have regarded it as itself a subtle fluid; others have regarded it as a vibration propagated from the illuminating body. A book on familiar science which I lately saw, defined light as the 'rapid undulations of a fluid called ether, made sensible to the eye by striking on the optic nerve, as sound is produced by undulations of air striking on the ear.' The same book added in a note, 'This theory of light is not altogether satisfactory, but has been given as the most plausible hitherto propounded.' I think, however, we will not perplex ourselves just now about the question what light is. We will leave that for the philosophers to settle."

"Oh yes, aunt Fanny," exclaimed little Samuel, "I cannot understand what that book says. Please skip that, and tell us something easy and interesting about light. You can always tell us something interesting, no matter what it is we talk about."

"Thank you, master Samuel, but it is because every thing God has made is full of interest, if we will only take the requisite pains to observe and study his works. Well, the first thing I will tell you about it is that, like all other things we know of, light takes time to travel."

"Why, then," asked Willie, "do we never see it move?"

"Because, Willie, it moves so fast that our senses cannot take note of its motion. The ancients believed it to be propagated from the sun and other luminous bodies instantaneously to the vastest distances.

But modern science has not only detected its motion, but has measured its rapidity. Now how fast do you suppose that light travels?

You know that when a railroad car goes fifty miles an hour we think it is prodigiously rapid in its motion. A ball fired from a cannon cannot be made to go faster than at the rate of about five hundred miles per hour. Yet light actually travels at the rate of two hundred thousand miles per second, or, in other words, passes over a distance equal to eight times around the world while you can count *one*. Hence it takes each ray of light a little less than eight minutes to reach our earth in coming from the sun."

"What a wonderful traveller,"

said Archie. "I shall hereafter feel more respect for the sunshine. I read lately in Milton's Paradise Lost, that the angel Uriel came from heaven to earth riding upon a sunbeam. What a swift journey he must have made:"

"Yes," said aunt Fanny, "that was the very idea which the poet desired to convey to his readers. The riding upon the sunbeam is, of course, only a poetic way of expressing it."

"I wish now to tell you another wonderful thing in regard to light. If I were to ask you the colour of light, you would probably say it had no colour at all. Yet does every ray or pencil of light combine and contain in itself every distinct or original colour found in all nature. Modern science has found a way to dissect, so to speak, a sunbeam, and separate it into red, orange, yellow, green, blue, indigo, and violet. It can even tell exactly in what proportions these several colours enter into the composition of each ray."

"Why, aunt Fanny," exclaimed Willie, "those are exactly the seven colours which we see in the rainbow. After the shower had passed over, a few days ago, I sat a long while on the bank of the river, watching the changes in the magnificent rainbow which appeared in the sky. I tried to count the colours, and thought I could plainly distinguish just those seven."

"You were right, Willie. The rainbow is one of the most beautiful and extraordinary phenomena to be seen in nature. It is produced

by the sunbeams striking at a particular angle, upon the particles of watery vapour floating in the air, thus causing a dispersion of the colours. God has especially appointed the rainbow to remind mankind of a great and merciful promise which he once made to the human race. Can you tell me, Archie, what that promise was?"

"Yes," said Archie, "after the flood, God promised Noah that he would never again send a deluge on the earth to destroy mankind. We had the story in our Sabbath-school lesson a few weeks ago. It is in the ninth chapter of Genesis."

"If that was the case, can you not repeat to me the words of God's promise?"

"I think I can," said Archie. "'And God said, This is the token of the covenant which I make between me and you and every living creature that is with you, for perpetual generations: I do set my bow in the cloud, and it shall be for a token of a covenant between me and the earth. And it shall come to pass, when I bring a cloud over the earth, that the bow shall be seen in the cloud: And I will remember my covenant which is between me and you and every living creature of all flesh, and the waters shall no more become a flood to destroy all flesh.'"

"Right, Archie. I am gratified by your correctness in repeating. The very words of the Bible, once thoroughly stored in the memory, are an invaluable treasure for one's whole life. In the light of the Bible how significant as well as beautiful a sight is the rainbow. Whenever it appears in the sky, God speaks to us by it impressively and mercifully. How great a pity that so many persons have their heads filled only with silly or superstitious notions in regard to the rainbow!"

CHAPTER VIII.

LIGHT.

THE tea-things had all been cleared away. The evening was bright and lovely. Aunt Fanny called to her three nephews to get their hats and take their customary walk. They were no sooner fairly off than little Samuel cried out, "Aunt Fanny, when we were walking yesterday morning you began to talk to us about light, and were just telling us some wonderful things about it, when you were interrupted. Will you not go on now and tell us more about it? Ever since you told us how each ray of light combined all the colours in itself, I have noticed more the effects of light, and am surprised to find how many beauties it is all the time producing."

"Yes, my dear boy, attention is the great thing one needs in order to find the world full of beautiful things all the time. Every touch of God's hand is productive of beauty. It is only human sin which has brought ugliness into the world. But let us return to our theme. What was I telling you when we were interrupted?"

"You had been telling us," said

Samuel, "about the rainbow, and how God had made it a token of his covenant not to drown the world again. And you left off with saying how great a pity it was that so many persons had their heads filled only with silly or superstitious notions about the rainbow."

"I remember now. I have heard of a great many such notions entertained among the ignorant and foolish."

"Oh yes, aunt Fanny," cried Willie, "I remember that some months ago I walked out one afternoon with Robert Simpson. As we went along there appeared a beautiful rainbow. Robert was in a state of great excitement. He said his old grandmother had told him that whoever searched at the foot of a rainbow, where it rested on the earth, would be sure to find there a pot of gold. He was quite provoked when I laughed at his nonsense, and ran off over the hill to find the foot of the rainbow and the pot of gold. I think he must have run a long while before he found either. Just then uncle George came along, and when I told him what Robert had gone after, he at first laughed, but then looked sad, and said it was very wicked for people to put such silly and false notions into the heads of children."

"Your uncle George spoke the truth. It is very wicked to teach children falsehoods."

"Will you tell us, aunt Fanny," said Archie, "how it is that daguerreotypes or photographs are taken by the simple use of light?"

"I have not time, my dear boy, to explain the process minutely, but can give you perhaps a general idea of it. The light of the sun is capable of producing powerful chemical changes in certain substances. Among the substances thus affected, is the white chloride of silver. This therefore is spread upon a flat prepared surface which is placed in a darkened box or *camera obscura.* By suddenly removing the covering from the glass of the box, the image to be pictured is with the aid of sunlight cast upon the prepared surface. The chemical action of the light rapidly causes there such changes in the colour of the surface as to leave the image pictured on it. It is a truly wonderful invention, and is every day applied to new and more extended uses."

"You say, aunt Fanny," inquired Archie, "that a sunbeam contains in itself all the colours of the rainbow, and also that it is capable of producing chemical changes. Do you suppose that all the colours which adorn objects around us on the face of the earth are derived from the action of light?"

"I would hardly dare to assert it, Archie," replied his aunt, "yet I think it extremely probable. Were all light for a long time excluded from our atmosphere, and then suddenly admitted again, I have little doubt but the colours of animals and plants would all be found to have disappeared. When celery is raised in the garden, by heaping the earth against it, it is made white, *i. e.*, colourless. Any plant grown under cover without light will be without colour. All the beautiful flowers too, which so beautify the face of the earth, owe the variety and intensity of their hues to the influence of the solar beams. Something of this effect you can see every day in the sun's power to brown or 'tan,' as it is familiarly called, the skin of a child when exposed to the sun's rays. A little girl showed me the other day a ring of white skin around one of her fingers. The whole hand had been browned by exposure to the sun's rays, except the part protected by a gold ring. This part remained a clear white. This tanning is the result of a chemical effect of the sun's rays upon the tissues of an exposed skin. A comparison between the animals inhabiting the polar and tropical regions of the earth, and between the parts of their bodies exposed and those not exposed to the light, will shew that their colours materially depend upon the chemical influence of light. Thus God is continually painting our world with a pencil of his own."

"Do you suppose, aunt Fanny," inquired Willie, "that light has any connection with the health and strength of animals?"

"Most undoubtedly, my dear boy," she replied. "A house or a particular room into which the sunshine never comes is unwholesome and its air injurious to the health. All animals, man included, need to be much in the bright sunlight, and can never be equally healthy without it. And now, master Samuel, as I have answered many questions, I want to ask one of you. Can you tell me where the first light came from?"

"Yes," he replied, "in the first chapter of Genesis it is said that 'darkness was upon the face of the deep,' until God said, 'Let there be light, and there was light.'"

"Very well, my boy. Now I wish you to notice that light was

produced by an instantaneous exertion of divine power. The command which evoked it from darkness is justly regarded as the sublimest utterance on record. Observe now that while light was created on the first of the six days, the sun and moon were not set as 'lights in the firmament of heaven' until the fourth day. For three days therefore there was light upon the earth without the agency of the sun and moon. Then God called the present arrangement into existence, making the sun the great source of our supply, 'to rule the day,' by his alternate shining and disappearance. And to relieve the darkness of the night, he set the moon 'to rule by night,' she catching up a portion of the sun's brilliancy, and reflecting its beams, modified and softened down into our darkness. Yet a few rays come to us from vastly more distant sources than either the sun or moon, even from the fixed stars, the suns of other and immensely distant systems. And it is a very impressive evidence of the unity and omnipresence of the glorious Creator, that those rays from all these other and numerous suns are of the same nature, and subject to the same laws precisely, as the light from our own sun. The same God evidently made their light and that of our sun. How infinitely great and powerful a being is He, and how worthy our profoundest reverence. Thus is it true as Addison has sung:

> The spacious firmament on high,
> With all the blue ethereal sky,
> And spangled heavens, a shining frame,
> Their great Original proclaim.
>
> * * * * *
>
> In reason's ear they all rejoice,
> And utter forth a glorious voice,
> *For ever singing as they shine,*
> *"The hand that made us is divine."*

"My heart's earnest desire for you all, my dear boys, is that you may be able to love him and trust him as you ought, and thus through our Mediator Jesus Christ have him evermore to be your Friend."

"How gloomy and dreadful that chaos must have been," observed Archie, "when as yet there was no light at all!"

"Yes, indeed," replied aunt Fanny, "only there was at that time no creature on earth to feel the blackness of that gloom. It was of God's goodness that in the order of creation he made light before he made any sentient creature. But if now he should, in his wrath for human sins, withdraw his light from the earth, the horror of that thick darkness would become utterly insupportable. I have read of prisoners confined in a totally dark room, but supplied with everything else to make them perfectly comfortable. The Chinese sometimes inflict this punishment upon criminals. The effect is said to be invariably that the prisoner before long becomes insane, and soon after, if the light be not admitted to him, dies a horrible death."

"I think, aunt Fanny," said Willie, "from what you have said, the beauty of our world depends more on light than on any other thing."

"Undoubtedly that is true, Willie," said his aunt. "It is light from which the entire face of nature, its animals, birds, trees, flowers, landscapes, skies, sun, moon, and stars, derive all those varied and brilliant colours which make them so charming to every cultivated eye. I was profoundly impressed with this when I saw the sun rise last summer on several successive mornings, from the ocean. You can hardly imagine, my dear boys, what a brilliant, what a glorious sight that is. And another, which I think quite equal to it, is the sunrise or sunset on a prairie. These and a thousand other scenes of beauty and sources of delight are all given to us through the agency of light. I hope that in reading your Bibles, you have noticed how often the term light is used in figurative senses. I want you hereafter to notice that it is always used to represent something which is a source of cheerfulness, happiness, and safety."

"Yes, aunt Fanny," cried Samuel, "I remember that in one of my lessons I had a verse which said, 'Truly the light is sweet, and a pleasant thing it is for the eyes to behold the sun.'"

"True. And now can you call to mind some of those uses which the Bible makes of light?"

"I remember," said Archie, "that it says Christians are 'lights.'"

"Quote the whole passage, Archie."

"It is in Matt. v. 14–16. 'Ye are the light of the world. * * * Let your light so shine before men, that they may see your good works, and glorify your Father which is in heaven.' There is a text also in Phil. ii. 15, in which Christians are said to 'shine as lights in the world.'"

"Very well, Archie. Many suppose there is an allusion in this last verse to the beacon-fire or light-house which on dangerous parts of the coast was kindled to warn off endangered ships. Just so, every Christian ought by his example and teachings to warn men of the danger of their evil ways, and show them the only safe path to the port of everlasting happiness. Even the youngest of you, boys, may in this way be daily doing some thing to bless those around you."

CHAPTER IX.

LIGHT.

OME, boys," cried aunt Fanny, the next evening, "let us resume our talk about light. There are yet many things for me to tell you on that interesting subject. Indeed, I think we might very pleasantly spend half a dozen evenings in talking about it. When we left off last evening, I believe we had just referred to that passage of Holy Scripture found in Phil. ii.

15, which had led us to speak about the light-house and its uses. It was just at that point we were obliged to break off our conversation."

"Yes," said Archie, "that was the subject. And this very morning, in reading a book of ancient history, I found reference to a remarkable light-house of those old times, and was thinking of what you had said."

"Well, Archie," said his kind aunt, "I am very glad if our talk added any interest to what you were reading. But now I want you to tell us what you can remember about that ancient light-house."

"It was situate on the Island of Pharos, which was near the city of Alexandria, in Egypt. It was said to have been built three hundred years before Christ was born, and to have been five hundred feet high. It became so famous as to have given name to the light-house in several countries. In France the common word for light-house to this day is '*Phare*.'"

"And now, can you tell me which is the most famous light-house of modern times?" said aunt Fanny.

"I think," cried Willie, "it must be the Eddystone light-house, on a rock in the British Channel. I have read of it, I think, more than of any other."

"I suppose it is," said aunt Fanny. "It was first built just about two hundred years ago, and its builder, Henry Winstanley, perished in its ruins about seven years after. It has since been renewed four times, and is now perhaps the strongest

and most scientifically erected structure on this globe. Thousands of mariners have doubtless been saved by its brilliant light from a watery grave."

"How far can the light of a light-house be seen, aunt Fanny, by a ship at sea?" inquired Samuel.

"That will depend upon several circumstances, my dear boy," was her reply, "especially upon the elevation of the light, the clearness of the atmosphere, and the intensity of the flame. But I think I have heard of beacon-lights having been seen thirty miles at sea.

"Lights are so made that the name and position of the light-house can be distinguished by the mariner. For this purpose lights of different colours are used. Sometimes several lights are placed on the same tower. And very often a slowly and regularly revolving light is used. Great intensity is often given to the light by the use of large and highly polished refractors. A Frenchman of science, named Fresnel, has the credit of having invented the best kind of apparatus for giving light. Altogether, the light-house is a most beneficent invention, a most admirable emblem of what every Christian ought to be. But we cannot talk longer about it now. Can you remember any other thing which in the Bible is called a light?"

"In several places," said Willie, "God's own word is so called. For instance, in Psal. cxix. 105, 'Thy word is a lamp unto my feet, and a light unto my path.' The Apostle Peter also calls it 'a light that shineth in a dark place.'" 2 Peter i. 19.

"That is right. The word of God is so called because it shows us our danger, our duty, and the way of salvation. For such benefits the Bible is indeed among all the books in the world like the bright sun among the other heavenly bodies. Wherever it comes it brings spiritual knowledge, comfort, and hope, such as were never known without it. Wherever it goes abroad into the world this prophecy is fulfilled: 'The people which sat in darkness saw great light; and to them which sat in the region and shadow of death, light is sprung up.' Matt. iv. 16. When a church of Christ faithfully holds and exhibits the true doctrines of the gospel, it becomes a means of preserving and spreading that light, and hence is termed a candlestick, as in the first chapter of Revelation. Such a church was that of the Waldenses. All through the long and dreary night of the dark ages, it kept alive in its Alpine fastnesses the pure and blessed truth of God, transmitting it from age to age when all the rest of Europe was involved in the darkness of Romish superstition. Most appropriate and striking were its insignia. A candlestick bearing a brightly-shining candle, surrounded by the motto, '*Lux lucet in tenebris*'—'The light shineth in darkness.' See John i. 5. Blessed be God that in later days that heavenly

light has spread abroad over many lands, including our own. And blessed, too, be God that he has given both promise and prophecy in his word to tell us that the day is rapidly approaching when this light shall shine on every land.

'Nations, now from God estranged,
Then shall see a glorious light;
Night to day shall then be changed,
Heaven shall triumph in the sight.'

But can you think of any person, who in the Bible is called a 'light?'"

"Our divine Redeemer," said Archie, "was predicted by Isaiah as 'a light of the Gentiles.' Chap. xlii. 6. The Evangelist John also, chap. i. 9, declares respecting Christ: 'That was the True Light, which lighteth every man that cometh into the world.'"

"Right, Archie. It gives me more joy than I can tell to see you so familiar with the language of your Bible. Yes, the Lord Jesus was the True Light of the world. Many pretended lights had appeared before him—philosophers, false prophets, doctors of the law, false systems of religion—all along through the ages preceding his Advent. But they were all false lights. They were never able to show to fallen and guilty man a safe, practicable, wide-open path through this weary and sin-darkened world to another world of happiness and glory. This Jesus did. For him it was reserved to bring 'life and immortality to light.' Hence he was predicted, Mal. iv. 2, as 'The Sun of Righteousness,' for as the shades of darkness are chased away by the rays of the rising sun, so was the Son of God, by his coming, to chase away the intellectual and spiritual night of ignorance and sin from our world. Every year this process is going forward. This glorious Sun of Righteousness is rising higher and higher above the world's horizon. His beams are every hour spreading farther and farther. How precious is the promise! How cheering is the prospect! With exquisite spirit and beauty is it described in that hymn of our book, beginning—

'Christian, see the orient morning
Breaks along the heathen sky;
Lo! the expected day is dawning,
Glorious Day-Spring from on high:
Hallelujah!
Hail, the Day-Spring from on high.'

But there is yet another Person to whom in the Bible this title is applied. Can you tell, Willie, to whom I refer?"

"I suppose, aunt Fanny," replied Willie, "that you refer to God the Father. I remember that in 1 John i. 5, it is said that 'God is Light, and in him is no darkness at all.'"

"Your answer is exactly the one I wished you to give, Willie. Now I wish you to observe that while the Bible is represented as '*a light*,' and the Redeemer as '*the* Light of the world,' of God only is it said that 'He is light.' God, in his own essence, is knowledge, truth, holiness, happiness, everlasting joy, and life. He is the source from which all these flow. Except by his gift, not one of them could ever for a single moment be enjoyed by any creature. He is light—pure light. 'In him is no darkness at all.' He is not only holy, but he is infinitely removed from and opposed to all unholiness. If, therefore, we desire to have fellowship with God—to be his friends and enjoy his favour we must 'walk in the light,' hating sin, loving the truth, and following after holiness. So only may we have the light of his countenance to shine upon us, filling our souls with peace, and joy, and hope. Faint and unworthy are all the cheerfulness and beauty which external light sheds over the outward world, when compared with that which the smile of God can shed abroad in a renewed and believing soul.

"Hence, of heaven, my dear boys," continued aunt Fanny, "whence all sin and ignorance are forever excluded, when every soul among the saints is perfectly and forever sanctified, and where only peace, and joy, and holiness are found, it is said 'there is no night there, and they need no candle, neither light of the sun; for the Lord God giveth them light.' Rev. xxii. 5. Without the intervention of any secondary or lower agencies, God himself, dwelling in the midst of his redeemed people, shall directly and fully impart to them all that can possibly help to fill up the measure of their happiness for all eternity. My dear boys, my heart's earnest desire and daily prayer for each one of you is, that by embracing truly the redemption there is in Christ Jesus, you may without fail reach that glorious place.

"You once more see that all nature is full of meaning and instruction, when studied in connection with the word of God. Whenever henceforth you look upon the sun, moon, and stars, the rainbow, the beautiful lights, and shadows, and colours that rest upon the earth, may you remember that God has impressed a new meaning on them all, and may you have both your minds and your hearts open to receive the lessons he would by them teach you."

CHAPTER X.

LIGHT.

ONE bright evening aunt Fanny and her nephews were tempted to stroll farther and later than usual. In returning, they passed along the margin of an extensive and grassy meadow. The sun had sometime before sunk below the horizon, and the stars were just beginning to twinkle here and there in the clear twilight sky above them. They had been so earnestly engaged in conversation as scarcely to have noticed anything around them, when suddenly little Samuel loudly exclaimed,

"Aunt Fanny, aunt Fanny, do look at the meadow."

And sure enough the meadow did present a spectacle worthy of being looked at. All over its grassy surface thousands upon thousands of fire-flies, or, as the children commonly call them, "lightning-bugs," were incessantly emitting their brilliant flashes, each in his tiny way helping to produce a beautiful, vivid, and ever-varying illumination. It was a wonderful scene, and aunt Fanny and the boys involuntarily stood still in order to observe and admire it.

"You have told us a great many interesting things about light, aunt Fanny," said Willie, "but I do not think you alluded to anything like this. Won't you tell us how these insects make such flashes of light?"

"I will try, my dear Willie," said his kind aunt, "but it may not be very easy. The fire-fly is enabled to do this by the presence of phosphorus along the under side of the hinder part of its body. Phosphorus will shine only when brought into contact with the oxygen of the atmosphere. The great and good Creator, besides furnishing a supply of the phosphorus to this particular insect, has likewise given it an apparatus which can be moved at its will, by moving which, the oxygen is admitted suddenly to the phosphorus, thus causing the light you see. These little creatures are particularly active and luminous after slight showers of rain. Naturalists say that this curious provision is for the purpose of guiding the fire-fly to his mate. In the United States these little insects abound everywhere during the summer months, and by such brilliant illuminations as you now see, give oftentimes great beauty and life to the evening landscape. In Europe the fire-fly is unknown, but there is in its place a glow-worm, which is the wingless female of another insect of this same genus. But they are few in numbers and of little beauty when compared with our fire-fly. Europeans in America often go into raptures over such a spectacle as this, which we are so accustomed to seeing, that we scarcely notice it."

Aunt Fanny stood silently gazing at the light-spangled meadow for several minutes, then raised her eyes to the stars.

"Shall I tell you, my dear boys," said she quietly, "of what I have been thinking these last minutes? It was, that the brief flash of the fire-fly is like the pleasures of sin, 'which are but for a season,' and then give place to the darkness of the night of sorrow and despair. On the other hand, the pleasures of holiness, the delights drawn from loving and serving God, are like the calm but permanent light of yonder stars, which shine on with unceasing and undiminished splendour age after age. May you all be wise enough to choose and secure the latter as being infinitely preferable to the former."

"Are there any other animals," inquired Archie, "which have the power to give out such light?"

"Yes," said his aunt, moving along the path homeward. "There are both plants and animals possessing this phosphorescent quality. It is said that in the coal mines near Dresden there are certain mosses growing in great abundance which are beautifully luminous. It is also said that certain species of fish possess the power of diffusing a radiance around them, but I confess that I am doubtful in regard to them. The chemical changes which take place in the progress of decay, both of vegetable and animal matter, very often, under favourable circumstances, evolve a phosphorescent light. Putrescent fish are often highly luminous. In passing through a dark wood in the night time, I have seen a decaying log glow as if it were a mass of living coal. Ignorant and superstitious persons are often greatly alarmed by this last appearance, especially if the decaying wood happens to be in an upright position. Such luminous decaying wood is often called 'fox-fire,' although why, I cannot tell."

"I have often read, aunt Fanny," said Willie, "in books about sea-voyages, of the fiery appearance of the water at night, especially in tropical regions, which is said to be very grand. What causes such appearances?"

"I am glad you have reminded me of that fact, Willie. Some years ago I had an excellent opportunity to see that spectacle, and it was as you have called it, a very grand one. I was passing by night in a steamboat from Mobile to New Orleans, over a portion of the Gulf of Mexico. The night was rather dark, although starlight. I had taken my place far forward on the extreme prow of the boat, to watch the golden sunset. My position was so agreeable, that I remained there, thinking of far absent friends, until the shades of evening had gathered over the great deep. As soon as it became dark, the waters of the Gulf, as they were dashed aside by our swift steamer, became brilliantly luminous. Do you remember, boys, our visit some months ago to the foundry in Johnstown, and how the molten iron poured forth into the workmen's ladles in a stream yellow as gold? Well, almost as yellow and brilliant as that molten metal were the waters of the Gulf of Mexico as they rolled off in great far-reaching waves from our steamer. But in addition to its brilliancy, the water presented spangles and coruscations of the most splendid appearance. Here and there bright golden lumps as large as a walnut, as they rolled away from our vessel's side, would seem to explode and be diffused throughout the mass like sparks flying from red-hot iron under the blacksmith's hammer. I was so delighted with the scene that I continued at my post, watching its ever-changing splendours until long after midnight."

"Oh, how I should like to have been there with you, aunt Fanny!" cried little Samuel. "But what was it made the water look so bright?"

"The phenomenon is attributable, my dear boy, to countless myriads of minute marine animals, which give out this light chiefly when they are disturbed by a passing vessel or other object. These little animals are most abundant in tropical seas, but are also seen elsewhere. I have witnessed somewhat of this same appearance on the water, when sitting of a dark evening on the seaside at Atlantic City, and watching the breakers roll up upon the beach. But it is only in more tropical latitudes that it exhibits its highest degree of brilliancy and beauty. These light-giving animalcules are so exceedingly minute that it is calculated that over twenty-six thousand of them may be found in a single drop, and over an hundred and fifty millions in a tumbler-full of water. Yet, so wonderful are the researches of modern science, that many of them have been figured and described by naturalists, who have studied them by the aid of powerful microscopes. And how glorious and wonderful a Being, my dear boys, must be that Omniscient and Almighty God, who created, who knows, and who sustains in its existence every one of this countless host of tiny creatures, just as really and constantly as he does a man or an angel!"

CHAPTER XI.

LIGHT.

UNT FANNY and her three nephews were walking slowly homeward. Above them, the clear bright sky was spangled with countless stars. Around them all was deep silence, except the chirp of the cricket and the vigorous duet of the katydid. They all felt the influence of the time and scene, and walked a long distance without exchanging a word. The boys seemed to be intently engaged in thinking upon aunt Fanny's last remarks. They were aroused by a quick and earnest exclamation from Archie.

"Oh see, aunt Fanny, what is that?"

Directly before them was rapidly passing a falling-star. It fell in a slanting direction from the zenith towards the horizon, and was distinctly visible for ten or fifteen seconds, when it suddenly disappeared. A feeling of awe seemed to arise in their minds, as they drew closer towards their aunt's side, and waited for her reply to Archie's inquiry.

"That was a beautiful meteor," said aunt Fanny. "Of what a falling-star is made, it would not be possible for me to say, probably there are many kinds of them, containing different substances. Natural philosophers have attributed some of them to the action of electricity, some to spontaneous or chemical combustion of gases in the atmosphere, and others to the falling of heated stones. Probably many are of the latter kind. Whence these stones come is another interesting question. Some say they were shot very high into the atmosphere by terrestrial volcanoes. Others say they are produced by combinations of gaseous and more solid particles floating above us. Yet others, and with most probability, contend that they were shot forth from volcanoes in the moon, so far as to get within the sphere of the earth's attractive force.

"Sometimes these falling-stars appear in great numbers. I remember that when I was quite a child, about the year 1832 or 1833, on a clear frosty night in November, there was a shower of falling-stars. For an hour or more the whole heavens seemed to be a scene of confusion. Thousands of these brilliant meteors were at one and the same time shooting athwart the sky in every direction. The ignorant were affrighted, the superstitious verily believed the end of the world had come, and the most intelligent observer could not avoid yielding to emotions of solemnity and awe."

"I am glad you have told us," said Archie, "that these are not real stars which fall. I used to think that if one of them should fall upon our earth, it might break it to pieces, or at least kill a great number of people."

"You are not the only one who has thought that, Archie," said his aunt. "It is one of the many blessings of science, that it can dispel a thousand fears which torment the ignorant portion of mankind. But it is the Bible only which can shew us the true and perfect way of escape from fear, by teaching that 'he who fears God, has nothing else to fear.'"

"Will you tell us, aunt Fanny," said Willie, "what it is that causes the twinkling of the stars?"

"It is their immense distance from us, my dear boy, because of which the fixed stars, even under the most powerful telescope, have no visible diameter. Hence only one stream of light from them can enter the pupil of the eye, and so vast is the distance, that the particles of light composing that minute stream, are at a considerable distance from each other. When a particle of light from a fixed star falls upon the eye, it produces a vivid impression, which becomes dimmer and dimmer, until another particle of light reaches the eye, when the vivid impression is renewed, and so on. This causes the apparent twinkling of the star. Hence in the sun, moon, and planets of our system, you never see any twinkling, because they are comparatively close by us."

"Won't you please tell us, aunt Fanny," inquired Samuel, "why it don't hurt my eyes to look at the moon as it does when I try to look at the sun?"

"Certainly, my dear boy. But I hope you will never try to look at the sun, or you may very seriously injure your eyesight. The reason the moon does not hurt your eyes is that its light is so much feebler than that of the sun. The light of the moon is said to be only equal to the light of one candle, placed at the distance of twelve feet from the eye, while the light of the sun is estimated to be equal to that of five thousand, five hundred, and sixty-three candles at the distance of one foot from the object. The lunar rays, when collected in the most powerful convex glass, have scarcely any effect on the thermometer, while, as you boys know very well, the rays of the sun, gathered through even a small convex glass will set on fire wood and other combustible matter. Willie, can you tell us of any philosopher who once did this on a large scale?"

"Yes, aunt Fanny," said Willie, promptly, "it was Archimedes. When Marcellus, the Roman consul, besieged Syracuse, where Archimedes lived, the old philosopher prepared curved mirrors, and so arranged them that by directing the sun's rays upon the enemy's fleet, the ships were set on fire."

"Very well. Now, Archie, can you tell me any thing about a celebrated statue in Egypt which was said to become vocal by having the light fall upon it?"

"Yes, I have read of it. It was the colossal statue of Memnon, near Thebes. It was said to utter a joyful sound every morning when the sun's rays first reached its lips, and a mournful sound when the sun set. According to the heathen mythology, Memnon was the son of Aurora. Hence the effect of the coming and going of her light upon his statue. It was a sort of joyful welcome and sorrowful farewell."

"Right, Archie," said his aunt, "several writers, both ancient and modern, unite in declaring that they have heard this sound, and philosophers have offered explanations of it upon very easy natural principles. Yet the whole story is of very doubtful credibility. But there is a hint which I think we may fairly draw from it. It is the duty of every living intelligent creature to utter God's praise in acts of devotion when the morning's light is poured upon the world, and when it is withdrawn at the evening hour. I have sometimes thought this story of Memnon's statue was invented by the Egyptian priests, to teach the people that if lips of stone gave forth a sound at those times, much more should the lips of living men become vocal, morning and evening, with acknowledgment of God's goodness."

"I want to ask you a question, aunt Fanny," said little Samuel, "about that star which guided the wise men who came to seek Christ, just after he was born. Where did that star come from, and what kind of a star was it?"

"Ah, my boy," said his aunt, "that question has puzzled many wiser heads than yours or mine. That it was no common star however, is very clear. Those 'wise men' or Magi, came from some country east of Palestine. The study of the heavenly bodies was their constant occupation, as it is now that of the professed astronomer. This 'Star in the East' was evidently placed in their view by a direct exertion of God's omnipotence. Somehow, probably by a direct revelation, God made them understand that it had reference to the birth of the promised Messiah into the world. That it was not a newly-discovered planet or fixed star is evident, 'for it went before them, until it came and stood over where the young child was.' God made it to shine for a special object. It was, no doubt, withdrawn again from human view, as soon as this end was obtained.

"And now let me ask you, master Samuel, if you can tell me where in the Bible, the Redeemer is spoken of as a star?"

"I think I can, aunt Fanny," said her little nephew. "In the very last chapter of the Bible he is called 'the bright and morning Star.'"

"That is the very passage which I wished you to remember," said his aunt. "Now to-morrow morning, if you arise early, before the sun is up, you will see that beautiful and blessed star which is made the emblem of our dear Saviour. It is worth rising at any time an hour before sunrise, just to see, admire, and reflect upon that 'bright and morning star.' How mildly and benignantly shine its silvery beams! How full of promise is its gentle light for a near and complete illumination of a dark and sleeping world! Learn to love the morning-star, my boys, as one of the most beautiful objects in all nature. But love to gaze upon it chiefly because it is recognized by God himself as an emblem of Him who is now shining as the Morning-Star of the moral and spiritual world."

Our little party were now approaching the house. The fire-flies were more rarely visible upon the higher and drier ground they had reached, while rising clouds had almost shut out from view the twinkling stars. It had become, really, very dark, so that it was with difficulty they groped their way along the well-worn path.

Our readers have long ago found out that aunt Fanny was most affectionately anxious to seize every opportunity to turn everything to account for the benefit of the dear boys entrusted to her care. They will hardly wonder therefore that she found even in the darkness a profitable theme for conversation.

"Can you tell me, Willie," she inquired, "what is darkness?"

"It is the absence or privation of light," he replied.

"We have already talked of light as a source of beauty in the natural world. Now can either of you tell me, boys, why the bountiful Creator should have so arranged his works that for nearly one-half of every twenty-four hours, darkness should cover the face of the earth, and hide its manifold beauties from our sight?"

"I think," said Willie, "that we enjoy the beauty of the world far more when we do see it by day, from the fact that it is all hidden from us so often and for so much of our time."

"*I* think it would be very difficult for us to get our sleep if we had no night," said Archie. "I remember in reading a book of Arctic travels, it was said that the long day of several months' duration became exceedingly wearisome and distressing to the travellers, because of the difficulty of getting their sleep soundly and regularly."

"And I think," said little Samuel,

"that a great many people would begrudge the time for sleep, both for themselves and their servants and horses, if they were not compelled by the darkness to give and take a regular rest. It seems to me very kind in God by making it dark, to compel people to cease from business and go to sleep at the end of every day."

"Your reasons are all very good, my dear boys. Many others might be added. God is very good to give us light as he does, and he is equally good when he withholds it. And it is just so with all God's mercies. Privations are usually disagreeable to us, but they are often God's choicest 'blessings in disguise.' If we are only numbered among his children, and are earnestly trying to walk in the path of obedience to his commandments, he has promised that he will make 'all things work together for our good.' Poverty, cares, sorrows, sickness, afflictions, death itself, will be made to accomplish gracious purposes in our behalf. When you see that by taking away the beautiful and serviceable light, God makes its very absence a mercy to us, learn to believe that whenever he takes aught else away, he can make its absence a blessing too. God's wisdom is very wonderful, and infinitely beyond our comprehension.

"Can you give me any instances from the Bible," continued aunt

Fanny, "in which God made use of darkness in working miracles?"

"Yes," said Willie, after a moment's pause. "He brought darkness over all the land of Egypt, because Pharaoh would not let the Israelites go."

"That seems to have been a very wonderful darkness," said their aunt. "It was probably intensified by God's power far beyond the darkness of our blackest night. It is described, you may remember, as 'a darkness which might be felt.' And then again, to make all the people as well as us know that it was sent by a direct exertion of God's power, while the Egyptians were involved in this fearful darkness, 'all the children of Israel had

light in their dwellings.' How terrible a concern must have been felt by the pagan Egyptians during the prevalence of this untimely and portentous gloom! And how beautiful and impressive was the ground for confidence and hope in their God, afforded to the timorous Hebrews!"

"There was another miracle wrought by darkness, aunt Fanny," said Archie, "at the time of our Saviour's crucifixion. You remember it is said that 'from the sixth hour there was darkness over all the land unto the ninth hour.'"

"Yes, Archie, that was a very astonishing miracle, and well worthy of careful study. You observe that those were the very hours when the Lord Jesus was passing through his dying agonies. They were also the middle or brightest hours of the day, being, as we would say, from twelve to three o'clock. Moreover, it is certain that this darkness could not have been caused by an eclipse, as some infidels have tried to insinuate. For this miracle happened at the passover, when the moon was always at its full, at which time an eclipse of the sun is impossible. No! this darkness was a loud call from heaven to earth, to take notice that its glorious King was suffering an ignominious death. It was also an expression of God's detestation of the fearful crime of those who, with wicked hands, crucified and slew his well-beloved Son. The miracle should teach us to avoid that wicked unbelief which led his murderers to slay the Lord of Glory, and to accept him in our hearts as our personal Saviour from sin and hell.

"While you will find light everywhere used in the Bible as the emblem of knowledge, happiness, and holiness, always of some thing truly good and desirable, you will, on the contrary, find darkness presented as the emblem of ignorance, misery, and sin, in their thousand forms. Satan is presented to us as the Prince of Darkness. And when the sinner, who has refused the spotless robe of a Saviour's righteousness, shall at last stand speechless and without excuse before his God, the order shall be given, 'Take him away, and cast him *into outer darkness*, there shall be weeping and gnashing of teeth.' My dear boys, whenever you look into the darkness of the night, think of the horrible and eternal darkness which is the portion of the soul for ever lost, and which must have been the portion of us all, had not a gracious Redeemer died to save us.

"But here we are at home again after our long and late walk. Look through the windows. How bright and cheerful every thing looks within! May we all, through divine mercy, find a bright and happy Home awaiting us in heaven, when we shall have finished our several pilgrimages through this dark world of sin and sorrow."

CHAPTER XII.

COLOURS.

ON a pleasant Saturday afternoon, aunt Fanny and her three nephews had gone out for a long stroll. After walking for half an hour they came to a shady hill-side, and having ascended a considerable distance, sat down under a spreading tree to rest themselves. From where they sat, they had a pleasant view over the meadow below them, and the opposite hillside clothed with forest trees to its very summit. Around them, among the scattered clumps of trees and bushes, wild flowers were growing in great variety and profusion. From the cloudless sky, the sun, yet three or four hours above the horizon, poured down a flood of cheerfulness and splendour over all the scene. All nature, down to her tiniest bird and bees seemed to feel exhilarated.

The three boys soon left their aunt, and engaged for a time in a merry game of hide-and-seek among the bushes. When they became tired of this they strolled about gathering tasteful bunches of wild-flowers for their aunt. Soon they seated themselves beside her on the grass, and noticing that her eyes were wandering thoughtfully across the landscape, they begged her to tell them of what she was thinking.

"I was just thinking," she replied, "of God's wonderful goodness, and especially how he has exhibited his benevolence in clothing all creation in such beautiful and pleasing colours. To the cultivated taste, the eye furnishes a feast of enjoyment wherever it wanders over his works."

"Yes," said Archie, "I often pity poor blind Tom, who lives in the village, and think how much he loses every day by the lack of eyesight. Do you think, aunt Fanny, he has any notion at all of the beautiful colours we continually see?"

"A man who has been deprived of sight by accident or disease may carry the memory of colours as of other things through his weary years of darkness," said his aunt. "But a person who was born blind, and who has continued so all his days cannot have any conception at all of colours. As this is poor Tom's case, he cannot have any idea of green, or blue, or red, or the difference between them. I remember to have read of a gentleman who taxed all his ingenuity to describe to such a blind man what the red colour was. After he had finished, he asked the man if he had understood him. 'Oh, yes,' said he, 'I think I do. It must be *just like the sound of a fiddle.*'"

The boys laughed at the blind man's idea of a red object.

"Don't you think, aunt Fanny," said Willie, "that it is a greater loss to be deprived of sight than of any other sense?"

"Yes," she answered, "I think it is a far greater privation. I have more than once visited the Institution for the Blind, in the City of Philadelphia, and it filled me with the deepest sorrow to see the scores of poor blind youth there collected, and to think that through all their earthly lives they could never see the bright and beautiful world around us, or have any conception of so many of its very choicest beauties.

"I have often thought, aunt

Fanny," remarked Archie, "of what you told us not long ago, that every ray of light contains all the colours in itself. I do not see, if that is so, how it is that different things around us come to have different colours."

"The theory is, my dear boy, that most of these bodies possess the property of fixing or absorbing some of these colours from the light, and of rejecting the rest. Blue silk, for example, absorbs six of the coloured rays, and reflects only the blue. You see that it is not the colour which the object retains, but that which it gives back to the eye or reflects which we regard as its colour. It is a part of this theory also that neither white nor black is truly a colour, inasmuch as a black object absorbs the entire rays of light, reflecting no part of them, while white objects reflect the whole and retain nothing. Both are, therefore, theoretically colourless. This explanation or theory of colours was first offered to the world by the great Sir Isaac Newton, who devoted much study to the subject."

"Please tell me, aunt Fanny," cried little Samuel, "why our old rooster and our turkey gobbler are made so angry when I shake my red handkerchief towards them. They don't seem to feel so when I hold up a cloth of any other colour. And I heard a farmer say, the other day, that a person attempted to cross his pasture-ground who had on a scarlet garment, and his big bull became furious at the sight of it. Why do these animals hate anything red so much?"

"It is because, Master Samuel," said his aunt, "our eyes are created with so much nervous sensibility that bright red or scarlet causes a burning sensation in them, which in many irritable brutes or birds leads to these angry demonstrations. Our eyes would be greatly pained by looking for a considerable time at a very large object of a bright scarlet colour."

"How disagreeable and painful it would be, then, aunt Fanny," said Willie, "if God had placed as much red as there is green around us on all sides!"

"That is very, very true, Willie," said his aunt. "The goodness of God shines forth very conspicuously in the selection of the colours he has placed prominently around us. The soft and delicate green in which he has clad the earth, and the still more delicate azure of the sky, never pain the most sensitive eye. Natural philosophers, after studying and experimenting long upon colours, have declared that these are just the two which are best adapted to spare and to soothe the nervous sensibilities of the organ of vision. You know that if a person is afflicted with sore or tender eyes he finds a shade of green or pale blue always best to shield them from a glare of light. If God had caused the vegetation of the world to be bright red or yellow, or even white or black, our eyes would be to us a source of constant agony. And that the colours he has given to the earth and sky are far more beautiful than any others would have been, no person of cultivated taste will ever deny."

After a moment, Archie said:

"I never noticed it before, but just look how many shades of blue there are in different parts of the sky. Up yonder is a large patch of bright azure, that feather-bed cloud off yonder is of quite a different tint, that western sky under the declining sun is different from both, and that heavy bank of clouds to the southward is of a fourth shade. I could count a dozen shades of blue in different parts of the sky."

"Doubtless you could, Archie," said his aunt, "at almost any time. While the general colour of the sky is blue, it is yet never wearisome through sameness, but presents an ever-changing panorama of colours and cloud-forms. It always makes me sorrowful when I think how very few persons love to contemplate and do truly admire this grand blue vault of heaven. I am persuaded that if they would oftener lift their eyes to admire the lovely canopy which God has spread above their heads, they would more frequently be led to loving and adoring thoughts of the beneficent Creator. But the same varieties of shades of colour may be seen on the green earth. Look across at yon hillside, and at those grain-fields down the valley, and observe how every tree and shrub and plant has its own peculiar shade of green. How dark is that of the pines and hemlocks yonder, how yellowish that of the chestnut and the sassafras, how silvery the tinge of the brook-maple and the aspen-poplars! So of the other trees, and so of the wheat, the rye, the oats, the corn. An experienced farmer can distinguish their shades of green when miles away. How wonderfully God mingles pleasing variety with beneficent uniformity over all his works!"

"I was noticing, the other day," said Willie, "when you were engaged upon your worsted work, what an endless variety of shades of the same colour you made use of, and I wondered how it was ever possible to make them. But now I see that we are looking at far more numerous shades of blue and green every day in nature, than ever I saw in your basket of zephyr-worsteds. And I see that as you used them to give variety and beauty to the piece of work on which you were engaged, just so God uses them to impart variety and beauty to his creation."

"Very true, Willie. And then in order to impart still greater variety and brightness to his works,

God has added brilliant colours, abundantly enough to please us without paining our eyes. Thus he gives us splendid sunsets, autumnal forests, gay butterflies, and above all, the beautiful flowers."

"But come, boys," continued aunt Fanny, rising, "let us go. We will continue this subject on some other day."

CHAPTER XIII.

COLOURS.

EN days or more passed before the boys and their kind aunt found an opportunity to take another walk over the hill. When they did, a marvellous change had come over the whole scene. The forest displayed, on every side, the effects of a recent severe frost. Many of its trees, so lately covered with green, now exhibited foliage of other and most splendid colours. The hickory and sassafras leaves were bright yellow; the dogwood deep purple; the oak russet brown; the maple light red; the gum and the sumac bright scarlet. Indeed each species of tree and shrub had now taken a new colour of its own. Only the evergreens retained their former green.

When our party reached the spot occupied during the preceding conversation, a gorgeous spectacle was spread out before them.

"Do you remember my remark, boys," said aunt Fanny, "that God had thrown in the brighter colours, sufficiently to give variety to the more subdued and chaster ones which prevail? Here you have a fine illustration of my remark. You are now enjoying a sight of which Europeans know almost nothing."

"Do not the forests in Europe change colour like ours, aunt Fanny?" asked one of the boys.

"To a very limited extent," she replied. "When the gorgeous splendour which covers our American hill-sides and woodlands in autumn is first seen by Europeans they are filled with admiration. I have heard that many ladies in England dress their hair with the bright autumnal leaves they receive from America. It is even said that the selection, preparation, and exportation of these leaves, of varied tints and beautiful figures, is becoming a means of obtaining a livelihood in certain portions of New England.

The ingenious ladies of our own country are also making more and more use of them every year in forming articles of taste and fancy for the parlour and the boudoir. But what, Archie, makes you look so grave?"

"I was thinking, aunt Fanny," said Archie, "of a text in one of our Sabbath-school lessons. I think it is in Isaiah, and it says, 'We all do fade as a leaf.'"

"Those few words convey to us a very solemn truth," said aunt Fanny. "Only a few days ago, these leaves were green and fresh, and looked as if they might continue so for months or years. But the frosts of a single night have smitten them, and these brilliant colours, like the hectic on a fevered cheek, indicate that death and decay have already begun to work upon them. Presently when the winds blow, they will be found loosened from the branches, and will be swept away to rot upon the earth. Just so it is with our mortal lives. We are here to-day apparently in full health and strength; to-morrow we are cut off and laid in the silent tomb. How infinitely important that we should be ready, through faith in the divine Redeemer, to give up our lives, however suddenly called to do so!"

They all sat gazing at the splendid scene for some time. Then the boys strolled off in search of flowers, and soon returned with a large and varied bouquet.

"How is it, aunt Fanny," inquired Samuel, "that the same sort of flower always has the same colour?"

"Ah! my dear boy, you have asked me a very hard question," said his aunt. "The distribution and perpetuation of colours, in the vegetable and in the animal world, is a great secret of nature. We cannot give a cause, except by referring to the great First Cause. Each of these plants is descended by a regular succession from a first plant of its kind, which sprang forth at the direct command of the Creator. Each plant has been like its predecessor in colour as well as in form and other particulars. *Why* this is so we cannot tell, except that God wills it to be so. At creation

God said, 'Let the earth bring forth grass, the herb yielding seed, and the fruit tree yielding fruit *after his kind.*' This law divine power impressed on every plant in the vegetable world, and it continues to operate until the present day, causing each to reproduce both flower and fruit of its own kind.

"So we see the same plant extracting from the earth, and air, and sunshine, often half a dozen or more colours, and arranging them with wonderful precision after the pattern of its species. Here, among the flowers you have gathered for me, is a *coreopsis.* It not only has different colours, but that half of every petal in its corolla, which is nearest to the flower stem, is a deep purple, while the outer half of each petal is a bright yellow. In some flowers, as in the pinks and sweet-williams you may see distinct lines and patterns upon the corolla. Now how the purple and yellow are made to appear on the same petal of the coreopsis, side by side, distinctly separated by the finest line only, is a complete mystery to us. But the works of God are full of mysteries.

"But I heard old David, our gardener, the other day talking about changing the colours of certain flowers," observed Willie.

"Yes," said aunt Fanny, "skilful gardeners have learned to do so by the application of chemical agencies to the soil about the roots of flowers. They can thus change the ordinary course of nature and bring forth the flower in new colours. I have seen blue and green roses produced by a skilful gardener. The hydrangea, the columbine, the violet, the pink, the larkspur, and many others are capable of an easy change of colour."

"But plants are not always uniform in their colours, aunt Fanny," said Archie. "You remember the little patch of striped grass in the corner of our dooryard. I have searched for hours to find two leaves alike, but never could. It is wonderful how diversified in breadth, numbers, and arrangement are the white stripes running through the leaf."

"And I never heard, Archie, of any one who had succeeded in finding two leaves alike. The striped-grass, or ribbon-grass, as it is often called, is a very peculiar plant. It always seemed to tell me that God is not constrained to employ uniformity, but can, whenever he pleases, work just as easily by diversities. There is no limit to his skill and wisdom."

"I have noticed, aunt Fanny," said Willie, "that in the Bible almost every colour is used to represent some idea. Is it not so?"

"Yes, it is so not only in the Bible, but in the general language and literature of mankind. And it has been so from a very early period. Can you tell me, Willie, what ideas are connected in the Bible with white?"

"I think the principal one is that of purity," answered Willie.

"Right, Willie, can you mention some instances?"

"On solemn occasions," said Willie, "the priests were commanded to be clothed in white, to signify that purity was required in the service of God. God will appear in judgment seated on a white throne, to signify the purity of his government. The redeemed will appear in Heaven in 'robes made white in the blood of the Lamb,' to teach us how absolutely free from sin they shall be made by redeeming grace."

"Now, Archie, what is usually signified by black?"

"I think," said Archie, "it is oftenest significant of wrath, or of the terror caused by it. The prophet Jeremiah said of a time when God would be angry 'the heavens shall be black;' of a time of great fear it is two or three times said 'all faces shall gather blackness;' and the place of the lost is called 'the blackness of darkness.'"

"And what can you say of blue, Willie?"

"Not much is said about it in the Bible, aunt Fanny. But blue was used in the curtains of the tabernacle, and the robe of the ephod was of blue. Our minister said one day that it was emblematic of truth."

"No doubt that was the significance of it. What, Archie, about green?"

"I suppose it signifies prosperity.

The wicked are said to flourish like 'the green bay-tree,' meaning that they seem to flourish. The Prophet Hosea likens the man whose trust is in the Lord to a tree whose 'leaf shall be green,' to teach that he shall prosper."

"Once more, Willie, what of red, crimson, and scarlet?"

"I think they signify violence, bloodshed, and crime. A red horse is often used in prophesying coming war. The Messiah is predicted as coming from Bozrah 'red in his apparel,' to indicate that he comes to inflict vengeance on his enemies. God promises pardon and cleansing to the believing, although their sins 'be as scarlet' or 'red like crimson,' that is, the most heinous sins, such as murder."

"Very well, boys," said aunt Fanny. "Now it is time for us to move homeward. You love to look at beautiful paintings. The Infinite Artist of the universe has placed all around you more exquisite specimens by far than any which man ever made. The most admirable paintings ever produced, are only feeble imitations of God's handiwork. The poorest of mankind is not shut out from the cultivation of his taste, or the enjoyment of the highest style of beauty, because he cannot afford to visit costly picture-galleries. Let him open his eyes and behold the works of God with admiration and praise."

CHAPTER XIV.

CONCLUSION.

UCH were the conversations of aunt Fanny with the three lads entrusted to her guardian care. Almost every day there was a pleasant walk by the little brook, or a ramble through the woods or over the hills, or a nice little expedition to gather flowers, or nuts, or berries. And when the weather was too wet or too cold for these pleasant strolls, they gathered in the family sitting-room. But whether in the house or abroad, their kind aunt lost no favourable opportunity to converse upon such topics as were adapted to interest her nephews, leading them to think upon the glorious Creator, and directing their thoughts from God's works to his blessed book of revelation.

And she had the pleasure of seeing her efforts crowned with a noble success. Her nephews were good and well-trained boys when they came under her instructions. Yet they were much like all other boys, having depraved hearts in their bosoms. They were not without many faults, and at times needed to be restrained, rebuked, and even severely disciplined. But she had unspeakable delight in soon being able to perceive that their characters were receiving a powerful moulding influence from her wise instructions and her loving counsels.

We have given but a few specimens of her conversations. As weeks and months sped on, she was delighted to find their minds awakened more and more to perceive not only manifold beauties in the works of God, but abounding evidences of the divine skill and goodness. Every day they would suggest to her new topics for conversation, while their questions and remarks grew more and more intelligent.

But she was far from being satisfied with this. Morning and evening she entreated her Heavenly Father to send his Holy Spirit to regenerate and sanctify them, and thus fit them for heaven. Every day she felt that the trust committed to her by her dying sister was not fulfilled until she had been enabled to lead the orphan boys to reconciliation with their Father in heaven, through acceptance of Jesus Christ as their Saviour.

One day, after she had been conversing with the boys she was exceedingly pleased to hear Archie remark, as soon as his two brothers were gone:

"Aunt Fanny, I have been thinking lately that if we, with our darkened understandings and limited powers, can see so much of God in his works, how much more must the aints in heaven and the angels see! and if this little world of ours which ıas been marred by sin affords so many proofs of God's glory, how much more impressive must be the exhibitions of that glory to those who are close around his throne!"

"Yes, my dear boy, the glories of those heavenly mansions, if revealed to us, would be far beyond our present powers of comprehension. But when God takes a redeemed soul to dwell with him in glory he no doubt prepares him for its enjoyment by giving him enlarged faculties and a clearer understanding than he ever had on earth. I saw, some time ago, some beautiful lines on this subject which I will repeat to you.

Since o'er thy footstool here below,
  Such radiant gems are strewn,
Oh! what magnificence must glow,
  My God! about thy throne!
So brilliant here those drops of light—
Where the full ocean rolls, how bright!

If night's blue curtain of the sky
  With thousand stars inwrought,
Hung like a royal canopy
  With glittering diamonds fraught—
Be, Lord, thy temple's *outer veil*,
What splendor at the shrine must dwell!

The dazzling sun at noontide hour,
  Forth from his flaming vase,
Flinging o'er earth the golden shower
  Till vale and mountain blaze—
But shows, O Lord! *one beam* of THINE:
What, then, *the day where thou dost shine!*

Ah! how shall these dim eyes endure
  That *noon* of living rays,
Or how my spirit, so impure,
  Upon thy glory gaze?
Anoint, O Lord! *anoint my sight,*
And robe me for that world of light.

"My dear aunt," said Archie, "I

have been trying to give my heart to the Lord Jesus, and asking him to pardon all my sins, and prepare me for his service."

"I am rejoiced to hear it, my dear boy," said his aunt, "more than tongue can tell. And has the Lord Jesus heard your prayers?"

"I do hope so," he replied. "I feel that I have a love to God and to the Saviour which I had not before. I sometimes enjoy a sweet peace when thinking of God and of his way of salvation through Christ. And oh! aunt Fanny, when I think of how much he did and suffered for our salvation, I want to give my whole life and strength to his service. I want to tell everybody what a glorious Saviour he is."

"I thank God," exclaimed his aunt, "for his goodness and mercy. And now, dear Archie, we must give him no rest until your brothers are both brought to look to him as their Saviour."

Nor was it long before aunt Fanny had reason to hope that her prayer was fully answered. Willie was naturally a far more thoughtless and less impressible boy than Archie. But before that year closed, he too seemed to have been reached by the influences of God's Spirit, and avowed to his aunt that he had chosen "the good part."

Dear little Samuel also, in his childish way, expressed his desire to be a child of God like his namesake of old and like good King

Josiah, and gave many sweet little evidences that renewing grace was working upon his heart.

And now we must say good-bye to aunt Fanny and her nephews. Feeling that she has the Almighty God to be her helper in the work, she has braced herself up with renewed courage and zeal to train the orphan boys for the Redeemer's service.

Archie has devoted himself to that noblest of all professions, the ministry of the Gospel, and looks forward hopefully to the day when he can proclaim to his dying fellow-men the glad news of salvation through Jesus Christ.

What his brothers will do or become, is not certain. But under the guidance of God's blessed Spirit, and the judicious instructions of aunt Fanny, they will, we may hope, do well whatever they undertake, and live for God's glory and the good of mankind.

www.ingramcontent.com/pod-product-compliance
Lightning Source LLC
LaVergne TN
LVHW050512100826
845148LV00002B/306

* 9 7 8 1 4 2 5 5 2 1 8 3 7 *